'Josh is a friend I trust, a ... and a soul searcher, so to ... understatement. I am delighted to report that every single page is a gift to your soul. It made my heart soar and my brain engage, and it made tears spontaneously fall from my eyes as I nodded along in agreement. *Something You Once Knew* will make you want to embrace every ounce of creativity you have inside and turn it into a piece of art, but importantly, it will show you that you already have the courage to reveal it to the world. Every human should read this masterpiece (and I don't call it that lightly) as I honestly think it has the ability to make us all better people.'
Zoe Clark-Coates MBE

'Joshua Luke Smith is an exceptional wordsmith. He writes with such wisdom and passion, and I know this book will be a help to so many.'
Guvna B, author and rapper

'The creative life can be overwhelming, deep and dark and yet rewarding, transcendent and everything in between. In this book, Joshua just went and made it even more approachable.'
Jake Isaac, singer-songwriter

'Joshua reminds me that, in dark times, wonder keeps our minds open, engagement keeps our hands open and reconciliation keeps our hearts open. The impulse to shut down is strong these days, but the well-told story shared by a beautiful poet may yet outshine our dismay. Thanks, Josh; I needed this.'
Bradley Jersak, Dean of Theology and Culture, St Stephen's University, New Brunswick

'Joshua Luke Smith writes with an electric heart-on-sleeve honesty that makes me feel like I'm reconnecting with a long-lost friend. Page after page, I feel the stirring of a mysterious wonder that I'm afraid I'd long forgotten.'
John Mark McMillan

'Joshua's tone and message communicate a wisdom that can only come from first-hand experience. The grace and poetic writing within this book will stay with you for ever.'
Propaganda, author, poet and political activist

'Joshua Luke Smith is both a skilled poet and a dangerous dreamer. His whole aura emanates a deep and sincere hopefulness and, just like Joshua himself, every line of this wonderful book is dangerously hopeful.

'Bravo Joshua.'
Carlos A. Rodríguez, founder of The Happy Givers

'Joshua writes so as to let no word fall to the ground. *Something You Once Knew* is void of any throwaway thoughts and sentiments, as Josh gently piques the appetite for forgotten practices you want to re-cultivate, and new habits you want to form.

'Josh's stories and unpacking of his thoughts unfold in a way that demanded me to slow the pace of reading, so as to grasp the fullness of each concept and invitation. I didn't want to miss anything. This slowing down, for me, was the exhale I needed in a world full of words and ideas hurled around at the greatest of speeds. This book is confronting without being exposing, it's challenging without pointing the finger.

'*Something You Once Knew*, for me, has become a book I want to reread periodically, when I need my North Star to shine a bit brighter in the sky, or when I need to remember my deeper whys and when I want to strengthen my desire for the road less travelled.'
Bianca Rose, singer-songwriter

'Joshua Luke Smith has given us a beautiful book. With the skill of an artist, the heart of a disciple and the vision of prophet, he invites us to encounter the grace of God in a way that stokes the deeper fire our hearts are aching for in these broken times. What a gift.'
Jon Tyson, author and pastor, Church.nyc

Joshua Luke Smith is a British pastor, poet and producer. He is the founder of Orphan No More, a creative community and platform for his own music and that of other artists. He also hosts The Pilgrimage Podcast and has given a TEDx Talk, speaks regularly at festivals in the UK and USA and has been featured on Complex and BBC Radio 1. He is married to Kara, and together they share a daughter called Eden. *Something You Once Knew* is his debut book.

This book is dedicated to Eden, aka Chookie,
my daughter and my guide.
You have reminded me of how truly
wonderful it is to be here.
I want to be like you when I grow up.

To my late grandfathers, Tiggy and Grumpy,
whose love of literature and storytelling led
my young heart to fall in love with words
and the worlds that they create.

SOMETHING
YOU ONCE KNEW

Waking up to the extraordinary
in your ordinary life

Joshua Luke Smith

FORM

First published in Great Britain in 2022

Form
36 Causton Street
London SW1P 4ST
www.spck.org.uk

British Library Cataloguing-in-Publication Data
A catalogue record for this book is available from the British Library

ISBN 978–0–281–08581–1

eBook ISBN 978–0–281–08606–1

1 3 5 7 9 10 8 6 4 2

Typeset by Fakenham Prepress Solutions, Fakenham, Norfolk NR21 8NL
Printed and bound in Great Britain by Clays Ltd, Elcograf S.p.A.

eBook by Fakenham Prepress Solutions, Fakenham, Norfolk NR21 8NL

Produced on paper from sustainable sources

Contents

Introduction   1

FOLLOW

1 The monk in the laundrette   9
2 Silence sounds like something   20
3 Finding the flow   32

BUILD

4 Take off your shoes   49
5 Oh, there you are   60
6 A dream within a dream   71

RECLAIM

7 The light in the tunnel   87
8 Lord, have mercy   95
9 I'm not creative   106
10 I am a temple   120

A closing benediction   129
Acknowledgements and gratitude   131
Notes   135

Introduction

It's so easy to feel like an awkward, uninvited guest at the party of your own life.

As well as recording and touring music, I worked as a pastor throughout my twenties, which, among many things, allowed me to walk alongside people, creating a space for processing and exploring the big questions and everyday realities that really make up our lives. I've found that so many people (myself included) go throughout their day not entirely sure whether they're meant to be here. It's as if we're awaiting a particular moment of validation, whether vocational or relational, that will provide the sense of belonging and wholeness we crave.

The truth is, that moment may never come and, if it does, it's probably fleeting. To quote the modern mystic Jim Carrey: 'I think everybody should get rich and famous and do everything they ever dreamed of so they can see that it's not the answer.'

What we need is a deeper truth about being here and being us. We need to stumble upon something ancient that is refreshingly new, a story that awakens us to the magic, the mystery and the miracle of simply getting up in the morning. We are here in our bodies despite incredible odds. The chances of our existing in the first place were almost zero – or, more accurately, one in a number too large to fit on this page. To quote Carl Sagan, 'Every one of us is, in the cosmic perspective, precious. If a human disagrees with you, let him live. In a hundred billion galaxies you will not find another.'[1]

However, arriving here, as impossible as it was, wasn't the hard part; it needed no effort or intention. It is the decision we make to be here, to remain and to say yes to the invitation extended by each moment, that requires us to choose whether we shall truly live by being present or exist in a haze of numbed indifference.

My journey into some of these realizations and revelations over the past decade has been through (what I've tried to summarize as) following, building and reclaiming.

To pursue the ancient art of **following** in our age, so entrenched with independence and self-obsession, is really quite a rare and radical thing to do. In following we learn to let go of our pride and face our shame, realizing that both are the expressions of a soul in turmoil. Our pride prevents us from confessing that perhaps we don't know it all and our shame hides us away, beneath the fig leaves of fear, terrified that we'll be exposed for being the fraud, the thief and the fool that deep down we believe we are. There are countless books out there about becoming a great leader, many of them are brilliant; this just isn't one of them. We're more interested in learning what it is to follow. In following we become a beginner again. Our curiosity transcends our cynicism and the world hums with a certain 'aliveness', as it it did when we were children.

It's so easy to consider the life you're living to be like the warm-up act before the band everyone came to see, waiting for something spectacular that only distracts from the significance of what is already happening. In **building** we choose to break the ground we're standing on and get our hands dirty. We choose the gritty, present reality over some abstruse fantasy land where nothing grows, bearing witness to the blooming of a garden, even here and even now.

In **reclaiming** we do the work of reconciliation. We seek out that which has been lost, stolen and forgotten. We create as an act of revolution, a rebuilding of what was torn down. We sing a better song, like Orpheus in the Greek myth, whose holy melody saved his fellow sailors from the beautiful yet deadly song of the Sirens.

There's an ancient scripture that says, 'The whole earth is yearning for the children of God to be revealed' (Romans 8.19, NIV paraphrased). Could that be true? As wild and ridiculous as it sounds, could it be that creation itself is awaiting the day that we all realize who we have always been and how unique the sound of our life is? Could we, like the majestic sequoia or the rolling hills of the Scottish Highlands, spend our days as an effortless announcement of God's majesty, a witness to divine craftsmanship, an unapologetic expression of what we were created to be and behold?

If it's true, then it's probably worth spending some time exploring it and, more importantly, what it is that prevents us from feeling as though our lives matter and that we have to be anyone but ourselves. We move through our days with an incredible tension: we are ticking off to-do lists, tying shoelaces, going to work, caring for loved ones, making lunch, and everything in-between. All the while, questions of meaning and purpose and angst and wonder rest below the surface and, though I can't promise this book will solve those questions or your existential crisis (in all honesty – it hasn't solved mine), I do hope that the time you're setting aside to read it, and some of the thoughts within, might create the space to give voice to those deeper yearnings and wonderings that so often get pushed aside in our busy lives.

I've never cared much for books that set out to solve something. What I find more intriguing is the unsolved parts of our lives. Like the awkward puzzle piece that's gone astray and yet, for all the frustration it brings, leads us to love and look more closely at the picture around the gaps, the mishaps and the unfinished parts of our lives.

That's why I've always loved poetry. Poetry is a space for the unvarnished vents and articulations of awe that we need to express. It's the soundtrack for our overlooked, unresolved and in-between places, and we've been doing it for ever, from King David to Kid Cudi.

I've written poems for as long as I can remember, though I didn't always know that's what I was doing. I've always been drawn to the thrill of writing, wrestling with letters, like that old story of Jacob, the man who wrestled an angel, fighting into the night, walking away with a blessing and a limp to show for it. And yet, despite spending the last two decades writing and sharing poems around the world – from a leprosy colony in India to a sweaty bar in Brooklyn, from Washington DC to a prison in Newcastle – if you asked me how to write one, I honestly wouldn't know where to begin. I'm no good at teaching people to write poems, but I'm passionate about helping people to see themselves and this world we're in as poetry, or as the apostle Paul said, 'divine craftsmanship', or as Albert Camus said, 'the hidden colours', or as Tupac Shakur said, 'the rose that grew from the concrete'.

We are walking works of art. Mosaics made of scars. We are stories being written and read aloud at the same time. Your life sounds like something and your life says something, and it's the hope in my heart that during this fleeting time together you might become more awake to that reality, more alive to those truths.

Everything that I'm going to share, I've paid for. I believe that words are expensive (we're going to get into that later) and so there's nothing in here that I don't speak to myself or hold to be true. These chapters are filled with my stories, but they are also your stories, as our lives are made up of the same things and our lives intersect with the same divine presence in whom we live and move and have our being.

We are poets, not because we learnt to use words but because we learnt to see the world as poetry. We saw something beautiful, redeemable and ultimately meaningful, and we couldn't help but give our lives to share it.

Let's begin, shall we?

FOLLOW

1

The monk in the laundrette

Never lose a holy curiosity.
(Albert Einstein, *Life magazine*)

I am what is known in some circles as an MK, aka a missionary kid. In the early 1990s, my parents packed everything they owned into two massive, dark blue storage containers and moved me and my big sister to Pakistan, where they would help to start to an eye hospital in the northern region, near the Afghan border. My younger sister was born there and my formative years were spent playing in the foothills of the Himalayas. It was an incredible childhood, not without confusing moments, as when the women in the markets would bend low to pinch my peachy cheeks, intrigued by the complexion of a blonde-haired, blue-eyed boy in their dusty streets. I can still smell the sweet spiced corn being cooked over fire, the powdered flour being clapped between tosses of chapatis in the air. I can see the man without legs who begged at the end of the street. My father told me it was likely it had been done to him as a child, because a boy without limbs collects more rupees from passers-by. I can see the wrinkled smile of the old woman at her stove, cooking rice and tandoori chicken, the creases on her skin as deep as the valley next to our home where the river ran for miles. Looking back I'm grateful that I witnessed such a mosaic of human experience so early on. We moved around a lot, which meant school was an ever-evolving expression for me and my sisters. It didn't matter much to me, I adapted quickly and enjoyed making new friends. It wasn't until we had moved back to England and I began high school that I locked horns with the restrictive formality and suppression of individuality that I found to be true in the classroom. I spent hours in the hallways of my school, exiled for being disruptive; I got into fights that led to suspensions, more out of boredom than anything, and I remember my mother crying on the way home from a parent–teacher evening after hearing about how I behaved. She said that she didn't recognize the boy they were describing. A year or two before ending high school I was diagnosed with what I like to call the triple threat: dyslexia, dyspraxia and dyscalculia (with a sprinkle of ADHD on top). This helped because I got the attention of a special needs teacher to help me navigate exams – you can imagine the mileage my mates got from that.

I left school with very little to show for it. I didn't have the grades to do A levels but I did get accepted into a local music college, though the theory and physics of music/sound went beyond me and inevitably I dropped out.

I was brought up in a Christian home but I wasn't sheltered from other beliefs. My father would play Risk with our Muslim neighbours on a Friday night, debating and dialoguing about their differing views while fighting for world domination. Our family holidays have always been a forum for discussion and discourse. I used to love listening to my uncles and aunts share their view of a world full of meaning and substance, beauty and love, without the presence of the all-knowing and powerful God that had always existed in mine. At 20 I was convinced I'd spend the rest of my life writing songs and poems and had come to realize it was curiosity that fuelled the greatest pieces, discoveries and ideas, and I couldn't imagine a better subject to study than Philosophy, which means the love of wisdom. Eagerly, I found a degree-level course nearby and readied myself to apply. Within minutes of scrolling through the application, I felt the crashing impact of hitting a wall at 100 mph. For my application even to be considered I would have needed to have studied Philosophy at A level or have similar qualifications in an equally formidable subject.

I sat at my desk for a few more moments, staring blankly at the screen with one deafening word ringing in my ears: UNQUALIFIED.

Who was I to think that I had what it takes to study Philosophy? How did I, a high-school failure, even imagine that I could keep up with conversations about metaphysics and logic, existentialism and enlightenment? Our world is built with words like that one. Qualified and unqualified. They helpfully distinguish between people and categorize us like sell-by dates on milk bottles. In a world where 'qualified' is king, it's no wonder those who fall at the first hurdle circumcise their curiosity and creativity for the purity of a mind that seems to work like everybody else's . . . even if it doesn't.

Don't get me wrong, I want the doctor who's opening my chest to be qualified to do it and for my mechanic to know the difference between a radiator and an alternator. I just know our brushstrokes are too broad and great minds, fuelled by nuance and creative passion, are abandoned by a system that simply doesn't know what to do with them. Einstein, arguably the most famous scientist of all time, was one of these people, revealing the need to acknowledge our neurodiversity. His son said of him, 'He was considered backward by his teachers. He told me that his teachers reported that he was mentally slow, unsociable and adrift forever in his foolish dreams.'[2]

As I stared at the screen highlighting my inability and un-questionable failure, I heard the whisper of a familiar voice, the sound of a welcome friend, meeting me again in my dis-appointment: 'Aren't you curious what would happen if you applied?'

I've known this voice since I was a child and I readily ac-knowledge that it's the voice of the Spirit. I don't know whether you have faith in a higher power, you have and have lost it or else are seeking new spiritual depths in your rela-tionship with God, but for me the voice of the Holy Spirit is my highest thought, indistinguishable from mere ambition or callous self-righteous reasoning. This voice leads me on a path back to my truest and purest self.

The journey isn't easy. More often than not it's costly, but when I follow this voice, it costs me who I don't want to be, it reminds me of what has always been true and inspires me to live accordingly. So when I'm invited to follow it, with all my might I try to, knowing that I may be led into the wide-open spaces of grace and mercy, into adventures and experiences I could hardly imagine to be true without it.

I filled out the application form, leaving a huge blank space in the section relating to 'previous education', and went about my day. I didn't think much about the submission after that and my desire to study slowly began to fade. As much as I was glad that I followed the voice and the curiosity within, I had come to terms with the reality I was unlikely to get accepted. It wasn't until a few months later that the whole subject of studying came back to the forefront of my thinking. I was living with a couple of other guys in a shared house and one morning our washing machine stopped working. Hastily, I made my way down to the local laundrette because, trust me, you don't want to live more than one day in a house of men who can't clean their sweaty clothes.

I stuffed my entire wardrobe into the metallic drum of the washer-dryer, pressed the option I wanted and then dropped in my coins, only for them to spill out of the change compartment. This happened a few more times before I realized that the machine was broken and so moved on to the one next to it. It happened again and again and, I kid you not, I tried every single one of the washing machines and only one was working. Frustrated at how long it took but thankful that I wouldn't be returning with the stench of my dirty laundry, I sat down with my then fiancée, Kara, and we started to dream about the kind of honeymoon two broke beloveds might have.

Within minutes of my soapy clothes beginning to spin, the door to the laundrette swung open and in walked a monk. I could only presume he was Buddhist since the robes he wore, top to bottom, were orange and the basket he carried was filled to the brim with other saffron clothes. We exchanged nods and then he began placing his garments into a nearby machine. I told him they were all broken, that it was only the one in use that was working, so he could either come back when the cycle was done or was more than welcome to sit and join us while he waited. He chose the latter and I'm so glad he did. It wasn't long before we were talking about the good stuff: religion, philosophy, ethics and the spiritual path. I told him I was the child of missionaries and had grown up around different faith traditions, that I was fascinated by the way we all see the world uniquely and find meaning and wonder within it. He told me about his journey in Buddhism, his interest in the ethics of war, violence and conflict in Buddhist societies. He told us that he was from Sri Lanka and we should consider it for our honeymoon. He talked of how he had spent most of his adult life travelling the world, writing books and even teaching at Harvard. As the conversation drew to a close and my washing cycle came to its end, he said, 'It's interesting meeting someone your age so interested in these subjects. Have you ever thought about studying it?'

I replied that I had only recently applied to study Philosophy but doubted I'd have any success as I didn't have the qualifications to get in. He asked me where I applied and when I told him he responded, 'How interesting, I am the Professor of Philiosophy at that university.'

A few weeks later, I received a call telling me that I had been given an unconditional offer, that my place was confirmed and it was time to get ready to learn.

It was the day I learnt that our curiosity can lead us to places qualifications don't dare to go, and just because you're unqualified doesn't mean you're disqualified. The world is bigger and broader and more beautiful than the systems we navigate, and the Spirit has a way of opening doors that no human can close.

It reminds me of the story when Jesus, walking along the beach one day, interrupts the lives of some fishermen with an audacious and slightly obnoxious invitation to 'follow him'. The scripture tells us the men replied immediately with a bold and unwavering yes, dropped their fishing nets and followed the wandering street preacher into a life they couldn't have dreamt of! This story has taught me so much over the years, I keep going back to it. It speaks to me of the invitation that the Spirit gives to each of us every single day, into a life beyond the one we're living. The story takes place around two thousand years ago on the shores of Galilee, an area known at the time for its religious activity and spiritual formation. The area was made up of active, committed, deeply religious communities. Children from a young age would begin memorizing the Torah (Jewish Scripture), learning their history and law at both schools and in the synagogue.

At 13, when their elementary education was completed, most students (and certainly the girls) stayed at home to help with the family and, in the case of boys, to learn the family trade, like carpentry or becoming a fisherman. It was at this point that a boy would participate in his first Passover in Jerusalem (a ceremony that probably forms the background of today's bar mitzvah in Orthodox Jewish families). The best students would continue their study alongside a trade, joining the adults in learning of the prophets and other writings.

They would progress from simply writing and memorizing Scripture to seeking out personal application and interpretation of what they were discovering. A very select few of the outstanding students, referred to as *talmidim* (which translates as 'disciples'), would seek out a better-known rabbi and ask if they could follow him, often leaving their families to live alongside him, surrendering their lives to become like him. It was a phenomenal commitment and an incredible honour to be accepted; you were far more likely to be rejected. I imagine many dejected hopefuls, walking upon the shore of the Sea of Galilee, head hung low, making their way back to the home of their parents, submitting to the life they were qualified to live.

The majority of teachers would instruct their students in reading, writing and memorizing the Scriptures, as well as communicating accepted reflections on them. A very few would bring new ways of understanding and interpreting the text. They would open up the Torah and bring an understanding that was new and potentially reforming. They would use phrases such as, 'You have heard it said . . . but I say to you.'

Jesus, we discover, was one of those few teachers who had *s'mikhah*, (a Hebrew term used to describe authority). He brought a new revelation, overthrowing the previous way of understanding and embracing a new and revolutionary way of living. He was referred to as rabbi by those around him: his disciples (Luke 7.40), lawyers (Matthew 22.35–36), ordinary people (Luke 12.13), the rich (Matthew 19.16), Pharisees (Luke 19.39) and Sadducees (Luke 20.27–28). Jesus fits the description of a first-century rabbi, especially one at the most advanced level, the one sought by *talmidim*.

Now let's go back to the beach. What do we know about these men mending their nets? We know that they didn't make the cut, they didn't pass the test and they weren't accepted by a rabbi as fit to be a follower. No one saw 'something special' in them, they didn't stand out and they didn't impress. They were working for their fathers, living the predictable existence that they were always expected to have. Then one day, in the distance, they see the rabbi Yeshua walking towards them. Perhaps he's taking an early morning stroll in the quiet of the day; perplexed, they see he's walking in their direction and, before they can think what to do next, he looks directly at them and says the most unbelievable thing: 'Follow me and I will make you fish for people' (Matthew 4.19, NRSV).

In just a few words he changes the narrative of their lives. The rabbi was looking for followers he could develop, people he could pour his life into in the hope that they would become like him. Jesus is saying to these humble, unqualified men, 'I see myself in you. I see within you the potential to become like me.'

They understood who Jesus was. Their 'Yes' was immediate because their understanding of him was accurate. It wasn't even a question, not for them, not for their parents, it was the opportunity of a lifetime, an honour reserved for the best of the best, and on that day it was theirs for the taking.

The Spirit calls us beyond the boats of our qualifications, the boundaries of our courage and the realm of our

understanding. We are invited to live a life we are fiercely un-
derprepared for, a life that will tether us to grace, free us from
our addiction to self-preservation and cause us to live in a
holy state of perplexity, enamoured with our own existence.

All we need to do is stay curious. I once met a woman doing
a PhD in curiosity (fascinating) and she told me that the
average 4-year-old asks around 250 questions a day while we
adults only ask an average of 12. What happened here? Did we
learn everything there is to know? Did the world become less
interesting? Or did we allow our cynicism and indifference to
suffocate our wonder? I've learnt that interesting people are
interested people. There's a direct connection between those
whose lives are filled with anticipation and awe and those
who live as though there's something new to be discovered.
Disappointment has a way of leading you to assume that you
know the truth about things. It's as if you struck the core and
realized that there isn't gold down there but plain old rock,
as if you know something everyone else doesn't but at some
point will. It masquerades as wisdom but it doesn't empower
or equip, instead it clips the wings of those flying towards the
sun that burnt you. The thing is, something really special happens when you remain intrigued by the idea that your first
thought – the one that disqualifies you, that one conceived by
disappointment – might just not be true. There is a world on
the other side of our fear, a reality beyond the illusion, awaiting our 'Yes', and the more immediate the better.

When you trust that Jesus reveals the true nature of
things, that there is goodness pulsing through each moment and kindness behind each door, you begin to live with

a certain open-heartedness. You live in such a way that you keep learning. You realize your experience, as valid as it is, isn't the only way of seeing the world and that you might live to be surprised by how wonderful being here really is.

2

Silence sounds like something

> Until I die there will be sounds. And they will continue following my death. One need not fear about the future of music.
> (John Cage, *Silence*)

During my time studying Philosophy, one of the many mind-bending, bewildering topics we covered was metaphysics, which, 'simply put', is the study of time and space, identity, possibility, consciousness, change, first principles and everything else that makes up our human experience. Within that module we spent some time exploring the dilemma of 'unperceived existence' (questions regarding the nature of reality and human perception) and it was during a lecture on that dilemma I had what felt like the most incredible realization. Our professor, in his patched blazer and coffee-stained shirt, proceeded to ask the age-old question, 'If a tree falls in a forest and no one is there to hear it, does it make a sound?'

Now, the reason this question has been around so long and its answer is so evasive is because it's a question both of physics (what defines a sound?) and of philosophy (what does it mean to be heard or perceived?). If you come at the question from the angle of a physicist, it's fairly simple to answer – no. The definition of sound, simplified, is a hearable noise. Since sound is created when something vibrates and sends waves of energy through the air into our ears, despite the falling of the tree producing vibrations in the air, if there are no ears to hear, there will be no sound.

And yet . . . the answer doesn't satisfy because there's a deeper vibration within us that seems to disagree with the notion that just because something isn't perceived it doesn't exist or . . . it didn't happen.

In his biography of Albert Einstein, fellow physicist Abraham Pais recalls one of many daily lunchtime walks with Einstein (imagine that for a lunch break). During their midday stroll, Einstein suddenly stopped, turned to Pais, and asked, 'Do you really believe that the moon only exists if you look at it?' Pais responded by saying, 'The twentieth-century physicist does not, of course, claim to have the definitive answer to this question.'[3]

The answer to Albert's question may seem simple: 'Of course the moon exists whether or not I look at it!' But it was a query that led to Einstein's effective rejection from the very group of physicists that he helped found. Pais' response represents the view that most quantum physicists held then and arguably do today: 'Existence in the absence of an observer is at best a conjecture, a conclusion that can neither be proven nor disproven.'

That is to say, from the view of the physicist, our existence is defined by whether or not it is perceived by another, or, the falling tree only produced sound if that sound was heard.

I remember sitting in that lecture hall enamoured with the question and troubled by the response. On some level I agree. I mean, I don't need much convincing to see that most people in our society (including myself) would seem to believe that unless a crimson sunset is captured and posted then it didn't happen, and unless a creative expression is viewed/listened to by millions then it didn't really matter. And yet there seemed to be a voice within me erupting in defiance.

No.

I cannot settle for a life that is defined by the reactions and/or presence of others. My life (and yours), like that falling tree, cannot be robbed of its impact simply because no one was around to see or hear it happen.

Which brings us to the philosophical question, what does it mean to be perceived? Yup, I know, this is getting a little abstruse and abstract but it's important because it has to do with very practical and tangible things. How we answer this question, I believe, defines how we live.

If we believe that to be perceived, like the falling tree, means being observed in a manner that is easily and scientifically defined, then how we live and create and express ourselves will be increasingly defined in response.

Don't believe me?

There's a reason we are addicted to our phones and their notifications. All those likes, alerts and messages, in a world with shallow definitions of what it means to be perceived, prove to us our own existence.

René Descartes famously said, 'I think, therefore I am' (in *Discourse on Method*, 1637). If he was alive today, I wonder if he would have said, 'My phone pings, therefore I am.'

As a race, we are driven to succeed not purely for the benefit of our society and the individuals we care for but also to achieve meaning and significance along the way. I know this to be true because I have lived it.

We're desperate to be acknowledged, complimented, re-posted, promoted, applauded and awarded because, in some strange fashion, it will convince us of ourselves. No wonder we're so busy hustling and avoiding space, silence and soli-tude if those very things seem to lessen our sense of existing.

When my professor asked that question, my mind went somewhere else. Perhaps it was because I knew I didn't have the intellectual stamina to keep up with the conversation, but I began to look at the image he put forward and see it differently.

Whether or not anyone was around to observe the falling tree, it had an impact. The ground felt it. That's undeniable and no amount of philosophical debate or scientific reasoning can change it.

Sometimes we're so concerned about who sees what we do or say that we miss the impact we have.

The ground was *shooketh*. It trembled under the weight of the falling timber and, as debris danced into the air, something changed. That moment mattered and the impact upon the ground was real. The same thing happens when you choose to own the fact that your life matters: it counts for something and there's a sound that only you carry, which needs a point of expression. Some falling trees aren't felt for generations, some impacts aren't acknowledged for centuries, and yet they shape our present.

I want to tell you about a man who has become a hero of mine. His name is Philip Doddridge. Ever heard of him?

From the moment Philip entered the world it would seem as if he was cursed, facing immense suffering at every corner. He was born still, believed to be dead and yet survived as the twentieth child of his parents. Yup, twentieth. His mother passed away when he was eight, and four years later he lost his father. I can't even fathom how that would have felt. He was given a legal guardian by the name of Downes, who promptly squandered Philip's inheritance, leaving the young boy orphaned and destitute at the age of 13. Thankfully, a Presbyterian minister, Samuel Clark, took in young Philip, treated him as a son, encouraging and equipping him towards his call into ministry. He went on to marry and have children but Philip would taste the familiar sting of grief when his first daughter, Elizabeth, died just before her fifth birthday.

Of his nine children, only four survived to adulthood. Let that sink in.

This is a man who knew loss, unrelenting suffering and staggering grief. Yet the water within his soul didn't stagnate. Philip Doddridge began to write, preach, pastor and equip. He saw it as his joy and duty to serve those around him and did it with flair, creativity and unwavering conviction. By his early death, Philip had composed hymns that are still sung today, he had written nearly 20 books, many viewed as classic Christian writings, and delivered numerous sermons that provoked and inspired, reforming a dreary, mechanical spirituality into a Nonconformist expression of wonder and hope.

Philip died from tuberculosis, his wife by his side. Immediately before his death, his wife noticed his lips moving. She asked if he needed anything. 'No,' he whispered, 'I am only renewing my covenant with God.'

Nearly one generation later, a young man picked up one of Philip's books.

William Wilberforce.

Ever heard of him?

I thought so.

I remember reading how when William Wilberforce returned to the shores of England after touring Europe in 1785, it was apparent that he was a changed man with a newfound conviction to follow God and a passion to fight for equality and liberation of those bound in the horror of slavery.

While on his trip, he confronted a spiritual crisis within his soul. Having led a privileged, hedonistic life until that point, something happened that transformed his outlook and, in a very true sense, changed the course of history. After doing some digging, curious as to what could have caused a revolution within a man so affluent and already influential, I stumbled upon the detail that Wilberforce had read a book while travelling between countries. The book he picked up, perhaps recommended by a friend, perhaps left in the cabin of the ship by a previous traveller, was *The Rise and Progress of Religion in the Soul* by Philip Doddridge.

The reading of that book led to the reformation within a man, which led to decades of activism, which played a central part in the abolition of slavery and the beginning of a new era for humanity.

I have one simple question to ask: what if Philip Doddridge hadn't written that book? What if Philip hadn't *followed* the internal invitation to give expression to something that only he could?

If we define the impact our life can have by who's watching now, we'll miss the impact that it's possible to have on people who aren't yet even born.

The writer of an ancient letter, recorded in the New Testament, stated that we are 'surrounded by such a great cloud of witnesses' (Hebrews 12.1), evoking the image of the Divine, alongside friends, family and the saints of old, cheering us on as we run our race. I know that's lofty and elusive but it's moving to think that there's another world, leaning in, holding their breath in eager anticipation of what we'll do next. More real than the 'likes' you may or may not get, truer than the reviews that could bring you down, more meaningful than the applause.

I spent my twenties working in pastoral ministry (among other things). That meant having the opportunity to spend time with all types of people going through a myriad of experiences, offering nothing more than a listening ear and some companionship upon the path. At 25 years old I had married, baptized and buried people. I was allowed into the hallways of their lives, the in-between spaces of grief and wonder, desperation and hope. I've lifted a woman who battled addiction every day of her adult life out of the mysterious waters of baptism as she declared, 'I'm finally free.' I've sat with a man twice my age whose second marriage was falling apart, searching for answers, longing for redemption, humble enough to sit with me, someone young enough to be his son. I've looked into the eyes of a woman who tried to take her own life, asking for a reason why she shouldn't try again and how tomorrow could be any brighter than today. I led the marriage ceremony of a couple who had given up on the idea of finding love, lost in the sea of disappointment, and watched them dance down the aisle together. I've wrapped my arms around a couple who lost their child, whose sobs pierced through my skin and touched my soul.

Bearing witness to the suffering and celebration of others has further taught me that our lives sound like something. No one moves about this world in silence, as real as that might seem at times. Your life says something and your life sounds like something, whether heard by many, a few or no one at all.

In 1952, avant-garde composer John Cage produced a revolutionary piece of music.

Kind of.

The piece is called 4'33" and it sounds like . . . silence. If you were to sit down at the piano to play it, you would open the lid, look down at the ivories and wait, for exactly 4 minutes and 33 seconds, and then you'd close the lid, take a bow and be on your way.

A year earlier, Cage had visited what is known as an anechoic chamber. It is a space that is designed in such a way that the walls, ceiling and floor absorb all sounds made in the room, rather than reflecting them as echoes. It's soundproofing to a whole other level. Cage entered the chamber expecting to hear silence, but he wrote later: 'I heard two sounds, one high and one low. When I described them to the engineer in charge, he informed me that the high one was my nervous system in operation, the low one my blood in circulation.'[4]

He heard his blood pumping around his body.

Cage had gone to a place where he expected total silence and yet heard a sound.

What this meant was that 4'33" was not a period of silence but an attentive capturing of the unique sounds of wherever it was being performed.

His pioneering composition speaks to the spiritual reality of our lives. If you are in the presence of that piece being performed, you are called to attention, invited to listen to the sounds that have always been humming below the distraction and disillusion. It is no surprise to the sociologist or anthropologist that in days such as these, so defined by those two realities (distraction and disillusion), that we are witnessing a re-digging of ancient wells, a returning to the spiritual disciplines of silence and solitude, which lead us into a fuller experience of our own 'being here', and it is precisely because they are of the most mundane and mediocre activities that they contain the most meaningful qualities.

Anyone on top of a mountain can exclaim in awe the beauty of creation, but to find the Himalayas hidden within, despite the hustle and hurry around you, to acknowledge in wonder the splendour of the person before you and to cry out a bold and trembling 'Yes' when the invitation to partake in your own story in all its imperfection once again presents itself, that is to truly live.

The average age of death in the UK is 80 years old. That's 42,048,000 minutes of life. That's the average running time of the song that you are living, and every millisecond of every second, of every minute of every hour of every day, of every week, of every month, year and decade is filled with the sound of you.

Like the description beneath a painting and the summary of a story, at the end of our lives people speak of the song we sang with our days. If you've been to a funeral, you've heard people articulate the way someone lived and the impression it left upon them. You don't need to know all the lyrics of a record to know that you feel something when it's played, and you don't need to know whether an image is painted with acrylic or oil to know what impresses upon your soul when you see it.

My friends, we are constantly creating. We fill the world with sound and colour without even thinking.

I remember sitting with a friend who had just started a church. He was manoeuvring around the nuances of leadership, hoping to create an environment where the congregation were challenged and inspired and his fellow leaders felt equipped and supported. It was obviously weighing on him and the tiresome act of tightrope walking was beginning to wear him down. A simple question came to mind. It felt too poetic for the type of conversation we were having and the very real practical scenarios that he was navigating, but I asked it anyway: 'You're leading this church. So imagine it's a canvas. What does it look like with the colours of your soul painted upon it?'

Abstract, I know, but I saw something click within him. It was as if he had permitted himself to see leadership as a creative act as opposed to burdensome bureaucracy. John Cage cited the work of his friend Robert Rauschenberg as another piece of inspiration for 4'33". Rauschenberg had produced a series of white paintings, seemingly 'blank' canvases (though painted with white house paint) that would change according to varying light conditions in the rooms in which they were hung or the collaborative display of people's shadows.

I love this so much. Our lives, like the blank canvas or the space, are being continually filled with image and sound, and yet so often we act as if we're not artistic contributors to the unfolding of our existence. You are not just drifting in a silent void of indifference. You are here and you are shaping the world around us.

Your life sounds like something.

3

Finding the flow

There is no greater agony than bearing an untold story
inside you.
(Maya Angelou, *I Know Why the Caged Bird Sings*)

I remember coming home after being on tour for a couple of
weeks to discover the flat reeking with the most putrid smell.
With my T-shirt tightly around my nose, fighting against
my embarrassingly quick gag reflex, I inched closer to the
source, anticipating the discovery of a dead rodent, rotting
in the kitchen sink, only to find a few inches of stagnant
water. As it gargled down the unplugged drain I remember
feeling amazed at how a shallow basin of water was able to
engulf the entire flat in its stench. Water is meant to go somewhere and if it doesn't it begins to smell. There's a word that
separates the murky pond that pongs from the lake which
invites you to dive in and break the crystal blue surface – that
word is *flow*.

Water that doesn't flow is dangerous. What begins as a harmless puddle becomes an environmental hazard, colonized
by mould and bacteria, the perfect breeding ground for
disease-carrying mosquitos and other undesirables. But the
water that has an inlet (like snow from the mountains) and an
outlet (rivers or streams) has the power to heal, hydrate and

restore. A lake made of living water can't help but create life within and around it.

Can you see where I'm going with this?

We're the same. We need to find our flow.

There is something in you that is meant to go somewhere. Every single night we go to sleep having experienced an un-quantifiable number of moments that shaped our day. Like water from the tap into the basin of our soul, we are being filled with emotions, informed by interactions, enamoured by thoughts, and all of it needs to go somewhere. Consider the micro-moments of a day – the first thought you had when you awoke, that first sip of coffee, the email you got with the good news you'd been waiting on, the conversation with a friend that left you feeling less connected than before, the tone of voice you used speaking to a colleague that you regretted, the mother and child you saw, which took you back to a day when you were young, the workout that confronted your lim-itations, and the meal you cooked, revealing you deserve a Michelin star in your kitchen. All of that, day after day, week after week, building up over a lifetime.

Jesus said that living waters can flow from the soul of a person. In fact, he said, 'Let anyone who is thirsty come to me and drink' (John 7.37). Imagine saying that of your-self, having the confidence that what is within you could refresh and restore, hydrate and heal all with whom you interact.

Before we dive deeper into that, a little riff about Jesus . . .

Christian tradition teaches, and as I have come to believe myself, that Jesus revealed the image of the invisible God. It is as if, before him, the Divine had been hidden beneath the cloaks of our human-made idols and distorted god concoctions. Jesus ended once and for all the Zeus-inspired imagery of a powerful but distant deity with the reality of the Almighty, co-suffering with creation. A God who was not waving wands or throwing lightning bolts but sharing our tears and raising a glass of the good stuff in celebration of being here in all its ugly beauty.

If God is the ultimate reality, the force that holds all things together, the Spirit in which we live and move and have our being, then in Jesus we are witnessing what this universe is really like, the mystery that had been kept hidden for ages and generations, the revelation of the Cosmic Christ, the character of our universe, expelling the lie that we exist in a cold, dark and indifferent void, revealing there is pulsing goodness running through it all. In Jesus we see a life of forgiveness freely given, restoring dignity to the downtrodden and love expressed in its most undeniable form.

Not only is Jesus revealing the true essence of God but Jesus is also revealing the true essence of us. Humankind, you and me. He shows how ludicrous the phrase 'I'm only human' truly is when uttered to make excuses for failure or incompetence. He shows us that to be human is to be miraculous, loving and compassionate, adamant that every person on this planet is treated as an image-bearer of God. To be human is to be a living, breathing canvas, decorated with divine creativity, a poem being written and read aloud at the same time.

So when Jesus says there are living waters within us, it speaks to something buried deep within the soil of our souls.

We have the potential to be alive.

Humour me and read that line again.

How many times have you caught yourself existing, drifting through the landscapes of your own life as if scrolling through your social media timeline, without being a witness to the wonder of being here? I'll go first.

A lot. That's how many times.

I learnt to drive late in life, I was nearly 30 when I finally passed my test after some pretty spectacular (and dangerous) failures. As a passenger, I'd use the time to grill whoever was driving on their technique and thought process, as if there was a trick I'd find that would guarantee success on my next test. To my annoyance, not only was there no magic man-oeuvre but most people said the same thing: 'I don't really think about what I'm doing, I often reach my destination without being aware of how I got there.' I remember refusing to believe that could be true. So conscious was I of my clutch control and mirror checking, how could you not be critically aware of every single movement you make? It wasn't until my first long drive after I passed my test that I realized what they meant. We set off and then, a few hours later, we were there.

All the moments and actions that I thought I'd be so aware of blended into one vague and undefinable journey. The more competent and comfortable I was, the less conscious and mindful I became.

So often when I ask people how their week has been, they get out their phone to scan the previous days, finding out what they did as if they didn't live it, or when I ask what music they are listening to, they pull up Spotify to scan through their library as if they weren't the ones hearing it. It says to me that we're getting really good at doing things and going places without actually being where we are.

We're getting really good at existing without truly living, and if you're not truly living then you're slowly dying.

I know people and *you* know people who, like the water in that sink, have become stagnant and stale and, if we're really, truly honest, they've begun to smell. I know it's true because I've smelt the odour around me, only to realize it's coming from within. It's only living water that doesn't stink; every other form attracts mould and disease, and so it is with us.

Living water, by definition, goes somewhere; it doesn't sit long enough to become a breeding ground for cynicism, envy or hate. When disappointment comes, and it will come, we're faced with an incredibly powerful decision to make. Do we allow this particular experience to define our universal reality?

Moving from stagnation to liberation is about finding spaces for expression.

Flow isn't reserved for the thespians, extroverts and artistically gifted. Flow is simply finding form for the story you are living, the perspective you see through and the unique temperament you've been given.

As I write these words on my laptop, I'm sitting outside on a brisk spring morning. I'm sipping a strong coffee from my favourite mug. Without the clay edges and curved walls of the cup, there would be no way I could drink the caffeinating goodness that is currently warming me from the inside out. Without the banks of the river, no running water would find its way from the heights of snow-capped hills to the depths of icy, alpine lakes. Without the carefully crafted pipelines that run beneath our homes, there would be no way to fill our glasses with the water that spills from the tap and 'hits the spot' after a long and tiring day.

So it is with us. And here's the good news and the bad news: finding form for your flow couldn't be easier. In fact, I'll put myself out there and say that you already know what it is because you can feel the invitation like an ache, a growing pain of creativity pulling you towards it and the living water it holds. The bad news is, only you can say 'Yes' to the invitation and whatever has stopped you until now isn't going anywhere.

There are two names for the 'resistance' (as Steven Pressfield calls it in his book *The War of Art*, a classic work on the subject[5]) that I want to address. The first one is disappointment.

I know a man who's angry. On the surface his life looks wonderful, a life many would long for, a good career, wife and children, but whenever I'd spend time with him I could smell the odour of resentment seeping through his words. I'd avoid meeting up with him and responding to his calls because I found our interactions draining and painfully negative. When I did finally pluck up the courage and patience to sit down across the table from him, I asked a simple question that I felt echo around the room when it left my mouth.

'What did you dream of doing as a man when you were boy?'

He looked at me and sighed, turned his face to the floor and replied that he had wanted to join the army like his father but, after numerous attempts, only met with failure and rejection. His life moved on, he went to university, met a wonderful woman, settled down, brought up three children and worked hard, but every day of this man's life he lived as a soldier without a mission, a regiment or a commission. He would sit at his desk, filing through admin, longing to be somewhere other than where he was. The death of a dream is as real as the death of any living thing, yet we move throughout our life without closure or giving expression to the hope we've buried and the desires we've laid to rest.

How many funerals have you been to for a dream that someone lost?

This man wasn't angry, this man was disappointed. He was grieving what hadn't been, and in a world that moves as fast as ours there wasn't time to confess, acknowledge or express the pain he had been feeling. There is no greater agony than bearing an untold story inside you.

In the Hebrew Wisdom book of Proverbs the writer exclaims: 'Hope deferred makes the heart sick' (Proverbs 13.12). Ain't that the truth?

The water within our souls grows stagnant and bitter when the brittle edges of disappointment begin to frame the picture of our lives. Disappointment, the ache of sadness that accompanies un-fulfilment, so often leads to disillusion, the sense that something isn't as good as you had hoped it might be, and from there, despair, the complete absence of hope, is only a step away. Creating flow revitalizes the water. It gives it somewhere to go. The only way a stagnant pond loses water is through evaporation, and evaporation only concentrates the pond's filth. That's what happens when everything someone says is tinged with resentment and bitterness: the conversation always returns to their pain and the world is coerced to fit into the lens of their experience.

Denying disappointment its power to define our expression comes with **following** the hope that things could be different. We don't do this through sheer will and callous determination but in treading softly upon the soil of our story, acknowledging the pain of what could have been and grateful that our disappointment, though full of ache and sorrow, has birthed within us a deeper and more sincere compassion for others. It is there that we shake hands with this weary and troubled companion, acknowledging how far we've travelled together but that we've reached the end of the road. Where we are going, disappointment fears to tread.

I love what David Whyte said on the subject:

Disappointment is inescapable but necessary; a mis-understood mercy and when approached properly, an agency for transformation and the hidden, underground, engine of trust and generosity in a human life. The attempt to create a life devoid of disappointment is the attempt to avoid the vulnerabilities that make the conversations of life real, moving, and life-like; the attempt to avoid our own necessary and merciful heartbreak. To be disappointed is to reassess our self and our inner world, and to be called to the larger foundational reality that lies beyond any false self we had only projected upon the outer world.[6]

When you embrace the form that beckons you, from book writing to ballet dancing, from baking to building houses, in the wake of disappointment, though anticipating the potential of pain and risking being hurt again, you are protecting your heart from a much more severe and fatal sickness – the loss of hope. When we create *despite* our past experiences, we give the gift not only of that specific form but also of our truest and purest self.

St Paul wrote that our suffering produces endurance, our endurance produces character and our character produces hope. How interesting, that our suffering, our longing, even our disappointment is a seed, not a curse.

The second expression of resistance I want to mention is **distraction**.

I wonder if you're reading this book alone? I don't mean if you're reading it by yourself but if you're reading it and only reading it, or whether you're taking one-minute breaks to check your feed, refresh your email or change the playlist? I only ask because I do the same thing. You don't need me to tell you that we're living through the age of distraction, but you *might* need me to tell you it's distraction, not some great incapability or lack of opportunity, that's preventing you from expressing what only you can in the world. Distraction seems harmless, mindless, without intention, the friend who's always got another plan to do the fun alternative. I have found, however, that distraction is not merely an *alternative*; distraction is an *anaesthetic*. There's a reason you're numbed or completely put to sleep before surgery; it's so that you won't feel the pain. A world without pain and suffering would be wonderful. I know we would all, in a millisecond, choose it if we could, but as you and I both know, it's not an option and the only thing worse than a world *with* suffering is a world that denies it suffers. Why? Because *suffering is a seed*. Our suffering, however great or seemingly futile, can reveal more to us about ourselves, the world we're in and the God who suffers with us than any other human experience. My friend Eric has suffered. In one year, he was robbed, nearly lost his daughter and buried both his best friend and his wife of 20 years. He is a man who has walked through fire and yet somehow doesn't smell like smoke. The fire burned but it did not consume him. He once told me about his perspective on suffering over a full English and it's stayed with me:

Josh, when my wife died, I was broken, I was distraught and I cried more than many will have cried in their entire life, but I learnt in that time to tilt my tears towards God, though they might be spilling into my cornflakes over breakfast. I was directing them towards God and so my tears became my prayer. My tears became seeds that I planted. I discovered that suffering was a springboard to intimacy, with God and with family.

Eric has taught me that there is no suffering so severe distraction can't make worse. The only redemption found in a situation so bleak, in a valley of the shadow of death, is to do as the Psalmist said and walk through it, receiving *the joy that overflows* as our reward. Given the opportunity to avoid, to reroute or to run away, Eric and others who you and I know have chosen the path of courage and most resistance, finding the hope that only those who have persevered in their suffering carry and give away to the world.

Distraction pulls us from the soft body of our own lived stories into the callous lands of fantasy and pseudo freedom. There is something that you're here to do, and if it terrifies you to do it, I'm even more convinced that it's yours to do. There's a really interesting verse in the New Testament, written by James, the brother of Jesus, who said: 'If anyone, then, knows the good they ought to do and doesn't do it, it is a sin for them' (James 4.17).

Notice the words he chose to use: 'it is a sin for them'. Not a sin against another human being, it isn't a universal moral failing; it is a specific disturbance of peace within the individual. Distraction doesn't just numb your pain, it also creates it. I know the feeling all too well of distracting myself from paying the overdue bill, as if, in some fantasy world it's going to disappear, when in fact, in a very real sense, it only gets worse. The interest goes up, more debt is incurred, the credit rating is affected and it can lead to the point (as it once did for me) that burly debt collectors turn up at the door ready to take your belongings.

> Jesus once asked a man to follow him and the man replied 'First let me go and bury my father', to which Jesus said, 'Let the dead bury their own dead . . . No one who puts a hand to the plough and looks back is fit for service in the kingdom.'
> (Luke 9.59–62)

I know, brutal.

Here's some context. Jesus wasn't speaking of some zombie-type scenario where dead people buried other dead people. He was addressing the reality of being physically alive but spiritually dead. In the first century, to say you were burying your father didn't necessarily mean that he was dead but that you were living with him, committed to being with him until the day he died, which in any case could be years. There was another practice of remaining near the grave of a deceased family member to then rebury the bones a year after the person has passed. Whatever it was, this man was simply expressing an excuse, a distraction to help him to avoid becoming a disciple of Jesus and sound noble in the process. In Jewish culture at the time, to speak of something being dead often related to being indifferent or uninfluenced by a certain thing or person (see Romans 7). Jesus was extending an invitation that required obedience, a reprioritization and a commitment that this man wasn't prepared to accept. It was an invitation to follow, to *be* influenced and transformed by the way and teachings of Christ. There will always be reasons to remain distracted, to delay whatever it is until tomorrow, but today is the tomorrow of the past. Why create any more suffering in a world so filled with it?

In the eccentric, ancient book of wisdom, the sage writer of Ecclesiastes penned these words:

> Whoever watches the wind will not plant;
> whoever looks at the clouds will not reap.
> (Ecclesiastes 11.4)

The whole book of Ecclesiastes paints a sobering vision of how fickle and short our lives really are. We are here today and then, like the grass or vapour, we are gone, forgotten by generations to come. Often, I think what stops us from planting and in turn prevents us from reaping is our belief that we'll live for ever. It will be soon, in the perspective of our human story, that a day comes in which no one on the planet knows who I am, and the same could be said of you. We aren't here for a very long time, our small patch on the tapestry of history is sewn quickly among billions of others. Our lives are meaningful, substantial and wonderful, but they are fleeting and we spend far too much time regretting and overthinking than we do creating, celebrating and bearing witness to the wonder of getting to be here at all, like butterflies who flutter for a day and think it is for ever.

A few thoughts to get started
You don't have to finish your life's great work by Wednesday, but getting started by then would be great.

This is what helps me, time and time again: **make it easy and take it easy**. Acknowledge the distractions, make a list of them so you can see them in plain writing. Perhaps it's a certain app on your phone, perhaps it's an environment you're in, perhaps it's a person in your life. Name the thing that seems always to be present when you know the good you ought to do and don't do it. The next step isn't necessarily elimination (though Jesus did say if your eye causes you to sin then gouge it out) but it is definitely limitation. **Make it easy** by setting certain times in your day when the presence of that distraction is completely and utterly absent. That might mean you delete the app (I delete social media apps and email from my phone whenever I am in periods of writing or deep work) or perhaps it's an honest conversation with someone in your life about the boundaries you need to put in place. If, like me, environment plays a huge part in your ability to be distracted, book in a time to be somewhere that inspires and evokes within you a sense of purpose and intentionality. **Take it easy** by acknowledging that you don't have to become David Goggins overnight. This can take time and you can start slow. I began my practice of writing this very book you're reading with a simple target of 15 minutes a day, which soon turned into hours and then a week-long stint as the love of and perseverance with the craft began to grow.

I met a woman recently who approached me at the end of a talk I was giving about some of this stuff and she told me, her eyes wide with excitement, that she had just finished writing the novel she'd be carrying within her heart for 30 years. She told me that one day she just stopped waiting for some unknown person's seal of approval and began writing.

What impressed me most wasn't the discipline and devotion she had so clearly harnessed to side-step distraction but her joy. It was evident that in the process of writing, of following, of finding form, she found herself, and there is nothing more infectious, attractive and provocative than a human being who has woken up that morning completely and unapologetically themselves.

BUILD

4

Take off your shoes

I feel God in this Chili's tonight.
(Pam Beesly, *The Office*)

My wife and I used to live in a tiny flat in the centre of the city of Bath. It was a really special time. We'd spend our Saturdays being tourists, going out for coffee, lingering over artisanal food and browsing the indie stores, buying more books than we could house or afford. Yup, it was the stuff that hipsters' dreams are made of. There's one coffee spot named Colonna, which was a stone's throw from our house; you might have heard of it, it's world-renowned. I spent more money there than on my rent each month and loved every minute of it. I remember one morning heading in there with Kara and our friends Marc and Amie, who are quite possibly the coolest people you'll ever meet, and when I say cool I mean effortlessly themselves in a way that makes you just want to take it in as if you know you're in the presence of something special. Anyway, we're hanging out with them and their gorgeous daughter Joni when this gentleman walks in and immediately gets my attention. He's magnificent. Not only are his trousers like a modern-day repurposed version of Joseph's technicolour dreamcoat but he's got the most spectacular beard. He's probably in his early seventies and so it's fully white, but it doesn't have a Father Christmas vibe and, if it does, it's the kind of Santa your grandmother would risk it all for, if you get what

I'm saying? Not a hair out of place but not overly trimmed to the point that it's lost its wild and rugged appearance. I mean, this is absolute bearded perfection. It only gets better. He sits down, opens the morning paper and after each sip of his coffee wipes his magnificent moustache with a handkerchief pulled from his shirt pocket. I rudely get up mid-conversation and walk over to him. I have to meet this man. I stumble over my words like a nervous schoolboy talking to the girl he fancies, with his friends snickering behind him. He tells me that his name is Robbi, and then I ask how he keeps his beard in such pristine condition and if he has any advice for a younger man in the facial hair game. He tells me simply never to shave it. Trim it, treat it, comb it, condition it, but never shave it, especially the moustache. He tells me the weight and character of a beard is held by the moustache, neglected at the peril of the practitioner. Surprised, I question how he's gone so long without ever shaving it. He tells me that he did once, at 17, because of a film he was in.

'Oh, so you're an actor?' I asked him.

He smiles, looks down at the table and, just before sipping his coffee and with a swift glance towards me, replies, 'I've been many things.'

I went back to sit with my friends, intrigued and star-struck from meeting a man I'd never heard of. Robbi got up to leave and, as he walked past, commented on how sweet Marc and Amie's little girl Joni was. They told him that she was named after Joni Mitchell, to which he said, 'I spent some wonderful time with Joni Mitchell', a soft and tender smile across his face. He became even more intriguing at that point. I asked if he could take my number down so when he was free we might catch up, that I'd love to hear his story and find out more about his life. He said he'd love to but would be away for a while, he was spending time in India and wasn't sure when he'd return. When I asked him what he was doing there, with one foot outside the door he simply replied, 'I'll tell you when we meet.'

He chuckled to himself and left. I've never heard from him since but our meeting, as you can tell, has stuck with me to this day.

There was something about the way he answered my questions that compelled me. It was like a village elder in the wild telling a younger man that his life was only just beginning. Instead of answering with what his job had been, he left space for nuance, mystery and intrigue. He didn't summarize his existence with a vocation, nor did he use the opportunity to impress me.

'I've been many things.'

I've lived a lot of my life waiting for it to start. I've spent time waiting for something to happen that's going to validate that my life is in motion, it's begun and we're doing this thing. Like sprinters in the blocks, waiting for the gun to fire, I've lived in anticipation of the bang, the firework that lights up the sky, for all to remember and commemorate my being here.

My friend Mike has one of the most creative minds I know. I honestly just love hearing him talk – it's like a live podcast full of interesting reflections and courageous ideas. I remember hearing him speak at an event once; he opened his talk saying (in his iconic Scouse accent) something along the lines, 'Tonight might not be spectacular. It might not be full of bright lights and fireworks, it might not take your breath away, but if you let it, if you choose it to be, it just might be significant.'

Dang. What an opener. What Robbi taught me in our brief conversation, and what Mike communicated before anything else that night, is that we're good at missing the moments we're living, in anticipation of what might be coming. In our infatuation with the spectacular, we're distracted from the significant. The words even feel different when you say them. The latter has a certain 'oomph' to it, like the sound of a bass drum at a live show, it's almost winding, it hits you in the gut. Spectacular moments come and go, they get the 'oooh weeeee' of a firework display or the applause after a performance, but they don't mark you like the significant ones. They don't leave an actual impression on your soul like a quiet chat with an old man in a coffee shop can. If I'm really honest I want to grow up to be like Robbi. I want to look back on my life as a journey made of many things. I want to be a man with marks left on him.

Without slowing down and actually being where we are, not only do we miss the unfolding miracle of our own existence but also there's really nothing of substance that we can offer the world. It's like inviting someone over for dinner but heating up yesterday's meal. There's a certain experience that can only happen when time is spent invested in what we're doing, through cultivating, practising and honouring what's at hand.

Distraction breeds stagnation. I know it, I've lived it. When I first started working as a pastor in my mid-twenties, I would see people back to back for 12 hours a day. I'd meet someone for breakfast at 7 a.m. and my final appointment would end at 7 p.m. I'd get home tired, frustrated and with absolutely nothing of myself left to give to my wife (thankfully, she's forgiven me for those days). It all changed for me one morning while meditating on the prayer that Jesus taught his followers to pray.

There's a simple line that reads, 'Give us today our daily bread.'

I'm not sure if Jesus meant that literally or figuratively but either way it struck me that there was a spiritual principle to be found through living in the grace of a day. There's no way I could offer anything of myself to the world, to the people I was pastoring, to the art I was creating, to the woman I loved, of any substance if I wasn't taking the time to acknowledge my daily limits and needs. Effectively, every person who came to me for advice or companionship as a pastor was getting some reheated lasagne from three nights ago. I decided I wouldn't give out anything that day which I hadn't received in the morning. That meant building margin into my life, space to discover the significance around me instead of frantically seeking the spectacular. If the words on this page you're reading ran from edge to edge, they would be very difficult to digest. The margin helps you to process what's on the page, and it's the same in our lives. The hour I have every morning on my own that refreshes my soul, the date nights and getaways I have with my wife to pursue our connection, the time I spend playing with my daughter that lights up my life, the

midweek solo trips to the cinema that inspire me, the spon-
taneous days out with friends and the week-long retreats I
take to create are the margins that everything fits within. It
puts the rest of my life in context. I learnt that being busy can
often be another form of apathy, a covert attempt to escape
the life you're living. Obsession with the spectacular moment,
the image of fulfilment we have in our minds, which comes at
the expense of being where we are, ironically, distracts from
the paths that might just lead us there.

There is an ancient story that speaks to this truth, it's recorded
in the earliest book of the Hebrew spiritual writing, Genesis.
The tale is of a man named Jacob, a cunning, deceptive soul
who was a gambler and hustler, a thief and as ambitious as
they come. His first crime was fooling his elderly, near-blind
father by dressing up as his brother and stealing the birth-
right that wasn't his. He soon had to escape town and run
for the hills, his brother in hot pursuit. Along the way, between the place he left and the land he was in search of, Jacob
collapsed, exhausted from being on the run. The story tells
us that he used a stone for a pillow and fell into a deep and
mysterious slumber. As he dreamed, it was as if his eyes were
opened and he fell into a trance, witnessing angels ascending
and descending on a ladder from heaven to earth. The experience startled him and when he awoke he exclaimed, 'Surely
the LORD was in this place and I was not aware of it . . . How
awesome is this place! This is none other than the house of
God; this is the gate of heaven' (Genesis 28.16–17).

How awesome is what place? This place? You mean this nowhere, in-between lay-by you collapsed into where there

wasn't anything more comfortable than a stone to rest your head on? This place?

Exactly. Jacob stumbled upon a truth, a deep knowing and understanding, that, if we're honest, we're all pilgrims in search of home. He discovered that the ladder from heaven to earth is leant against the in-between and seemingly mundane moments of our life. The significant is hiding in plain sight but with eyes blinded by the spectacular, sadly, we rarely see it. You may remember the story of Moses, a shepherd in the desert who, while walking the dusty plains he knew so well, caught a glimpse of a bush ablaze. Now, that in itself wasn't anything too special. Given the desert heat and the dry brittle branches, it wasn't uncommon for a bush to catch alight. What was more significant was that this bush didn't appear to be consumed. But what the rabbis consider to be even more significant was that Moses was walking slowly enough to notice and, as the scripture tells us, 'turned aside to take a further look'. As he approached the bush a voice spoke to him, saying, 'Take off your sandals, for the place where you are standing is holy ground' (Exodus 3.5).

This bit of ground? This dusty, desolate, desert patch, which looks just like the rest that surrounds it for miles, is holy?

Exactly. Moses spoke with God that day, a conversation that changed the course of history for the Jewish people, leading to an exodus, the abolition of slavery for a generation of people. You could say that it led to something undeniably spectacular, which he would have missed had he not taken notice of the significant hiding in the ordinary of his life. As the Victorian poet Elizabeth Barrett Browning once said:

> Earth's crammed with heaven,
> And every common bush afire with God;
> But only he who sees, takes off his shoes;
> The rest sit round it, and pluck blackberries.[7]

Let's go back to Jacob for a moment. A while later in the story, another strange event unfolds throughout the night. We're at the climax of his tale – the brother he robbed has caught up with him and this time he has an army. Jacob has sent his family and belongings ahead of him and he's alone, riddled with anxiety and dread. Just as he's beginning to contemplate his life and consider his next move, all of a sudden, out of the darkness, a man appears and for some unexplained reason they start throwing hands. The scuffle turns into a brawl that lasts the night and, as dawn begins to break, the man, realizing he can't overpower Jacob, pulls out a move not even Khabib had in his grappling tool belt and miraculously knocks his hip socket out of place. Still, Jacob holds on and with unmatched tenacity and endurance says to the man, 'I will not let you go unless you bless me' (Genesis 32.26).

What a strange thing to say to a stranger with whom you've been brawling all night. It's as if the hip-socket move opened his eyes to the fact this might not be a mere man he's engaged with. The stranger asks him for his name and, after Jacob replies, he tells him that he'll no longer be called Jacob but Israel. Jacob, still obviously somewhat perplexed by what's taking place, asks the man for his name and the response is some Christopher Nolan-level freaking genius: 'Why do you ask for my name?' Because he had already told Jacob his name when he gave Jacob his new name: *Israel* – which means 'the one who wrestles with God'.

Mic drop, right?

The story ends with Jacob naming the spot of the fight 'Peniel', which translates as 'face of God'. So Jacob caught up with what went down and he marked it. He recognized that, in the darkness of the night, in the valley of the shadow of his soul, he had met with God. He never walked the same after that night and his limp speaks to all of us who have also felt the pain of being out of place. Those who walk with a limp are often those who found something worth fighting for. The imperfection they carry is a display of the conviction and endurance they have. If God can meet us in the wilderness, in a wrestling match no less, then there truly isn't any part of our life so desolate or frayed that the Spirit can't intervene and make something new. The thing about wrestling with someone – and I know this from experience – is that, as violent and intense as it may look, it's intimate and it makes the other person undeniably unavoidable. Jacob had spent his life on the run, so it was fitting that God chose to pin him down. When you're wrestling with God, questioning your beliefs and feeling utterly lost in the in-between spaces of your life, know that you're in good company and a blessing follows the battle if you hold on and endure the night.

A few weeks after our daughter was born, I caught myself contemplating the fact that there had been an evening when

I went to bed and had enjoyed the final night of peaceful, uninterrupted sleep that I would have for months. How naive I was back then, how blissfully unaware of what was to come. In all honesty, our daughter has been an absolute dream and I have nothing to moan about, but those first couple of months will knock you sideways. The best parenting advice we were given was to find a light-hearted series to watch, something we could put on when our daughter decided the day would begin at 3 a.m. and there was no sign of getting back to sleep. We chose *The Office* (the US one, though I'll always prefer the UK one) and ploughed through those nine seasons in no time, kept in hysterics by Steve Carell's genius. There's a scene in one of the early series where the whole crew go out to a Chili's to celebrate their nonsensical office award ceremony 'The Dundies'. Pam, the office receptionist, wins an award for 'whitest sneakers in the office'. She gets up to receive it and thanks God like most do at the Oscars or Grammys, but then pauses and says, 'I feel God in this Chili's tonight.'

Perhaps it was because I was drunk with tiredness but that line spoke to me. There was something of a holy ludicrousness about it. There she was at a Chili's, where the food and drink are cheap and the interior is tacky and they're giving out awards for the whitest sneakers, and yet the ground is holy and God is present; there is a ladder to heaven leaning against the wall. It says to me that if God can't be found there, then God can't be found anywhere.

I turned to Kara and said, 'Let's use that as our mantra', and so we did. Each night when Eden would wake up, screaming into the blackness of our room, her voice bouncing across the walls, and we'd be changing nappies with poop getting on our fingers or I'd be burping her or Kara would be breastfeeding, we'd take a moment to glance at each other and say, 'I feel God in this Chili's tonight.'

5

Oh, there you are

We do not want to be beginners. But let us be convinced of
the fact that we will never be anything else but beginners,
all our life!
(Thomas Merton, *Contemplative Prayer*)

I spent a few years in my early twenties working in retail.
The shop where I worked at that time was Superdry and
underneath the logo it had some Japanese lettering, which the
branding team evidently thought was cool but, as a Japanese
customer once pointed out, translated as 'Super Not Wet',
which isn't so catchy. Anyway, I worked there full time, fold-
ing T-shirts and replenishing stock, doing what needed to be
done to pay the rent on our ridiculously expensive one-room
flat, which only had two doors in total, the entrance and the
bathroom. We had just got married and life was simple and
wonderful. Even so, each day on the shop floor I felt a growing
discontent towards a life that was like it needed some rocket
fuel poured into it. Kara and I would spend the weekends
jumping on trains and buses, lugging music gear around the
country, playing shows anywhere that would take us, from
tattoo parlours to coffee shops, and loved every minute of it.
But Monday morning would soon come around again and
the dissatisfaction would set back in. I just wanted to be 'out
there', on the road, playing shows and living out the dreams
I held so dearly.

Everything changed for me one morning, after a difficult interaction with a customer. I was reminded of the ancient wisdom of a Chinese sage we'd been studying in Philosophy: 'Wherever you go, there you are.'

Confucious wrote those words in about 500 BC and here they were, speaking to the soul of a millennial working in retail circa 2012.

It was honestly a life-defining moment that truly shifted my spiritual and creative paradigm. I suddenly became acutely aware that wherever I'd go in life, I'd always be taking me with me. Not only that but 'there' was only ever going to be another 'here', and thus the sense of there being someplace somewhere at some other time in your life that will somehow satisfy those inner longings is but an illusion.

Our lives are made up of a sequence of 'here and nows' and only when we live as though that's the case do we find actual inner fulfilment. I grew up in a spiritual environment that was intensely focused on the 'there'. There was always talk about the coming revival, a great awakening that would fulfil prophecies and prayers of old, and ultimately the return of Jesus, which would usher in the new era that we longed for. It was in our prayers, songs and conversations and, for all that was good and true about it, I was left with a deep sense that 'here' was no more than a means to an end, and over time it bred an agonizing dissatisfaction. I suppose on reflection that way of being always put God somewhere else as well, too busy for the day-to-day workings of our life, focused on the 'big picture', the apocalyptic narrative and end-of-days assignments. Over time that creates a mighty chasm and a real sense of aloneness in the world, a sense that you're behind or that you've missed out on the higher calling that was once available. That day on the shop floor led me to rethink things. I didn't want to take that frustrated, disappointed and dissatisfied soul with me into the future; I didn't want to arrive at all the moments I longed for with the same sense of underwhelming and not enough-ness I currently felt.

I knew I needed help and guides that would lead me on the path. Ironically, it was Confucius, the pagan Chinese philosopher, who led me into the mystical tradition of Christian contemplation, a whole world of thought and practice that I hadn't known in my Charismatic/Evangelical upbringing. I felt that I was being born again, seeing the world anew and rekindling my love for the evolving landscape of the spiritual realm. I started reading everything I could get my hands on that would teach me a new language and way of expressing my faith. The first book I read was Richard Foster's *The Spiritual Disciplines*, which blew my mind. He humbly led me into the practices that I had always believed were saved for the monks and holy among us, like meditation, contemplative prayer and fasting. Not only that but, through the pages of his book, he introduced me to St John of the Cross, Thomas Merton, St Francis and Julian of Norwich (among many others), whose writings I discovered and devoured. These mothers and fathers of the spiritual path were helping me to see that Jesus didn't come with a message of how to get 'there' but with a manifesto of how to truly be 'here'. Yes, he spoke of a kingdom that was coming but he also said that kingdom was within and lived a life with such joy and intentional presentness that the kingdom was manifested anywhere he was.

I remember feeling so compelled by the story in the Gospels about the woman who had been bleeding for 12 years and, with all the faith and courage she could summon, reached out for Jesus amid a crowd, touching only the hem of his garment. Despite the chaos and clamour of those around him, Jesus stopped, aware that something significant was happening, acknowledged her and made her well. How spectacular! It taught me that revival (the revitalization of a place or person) can happen every time we respond to the Spirit at the moment we're in. Looking back (and recognizing it in myself today), I realize that it's so easy to be lost where you are. I know it sounds strange and contradictory but how often do you find yourself in a moment where you have a sense of being untethered, disconnected and unsure? How often do you go into a meeting or even being with friends and experience an inner 'lostness'? It's as if, although we're 'here', we don't truly know where we are.

The Hebrew Scriptures begin with a story that perfectly captures this experience. The provocative and poetic writing in Genesis tells us that God would go walking with his friends, Adam and Eve, in the cool of the day. Imagine that, after the sun had been in full heat when the air was cooling down, the divine Gardener would revel in his creation with those he created, admiring its beauty and enjoying spending time with one another. One day, God comes to the garden but Adam and Eve are nowhere to be seen. The story tells us that they have been tricked into believing they could become like God and disobeyed the one thing they were warned not to do. In their shame and humiliation they have hidden and so God called out, into the cool of the day, 'Where are you?' Of course, it is not God who has lost them, he knows where they are and he knows what they have done. It is they who have lost themselves, and God seeks to find them.

What a powerful question that is: *'Where are you?'*

The answer may seem obvious: you're wherever you're sitting reading this book right now. But there is a deeper and truer way of locating ourselves that reconnects us with the present moment we're in and the God who is always seeking to find us. Where you are is defined by what's around you. When you depend on GPS to get you somewhere, it wouldn't suffice just to open up your map app and see the pulsing blue dot, you need the context of the terrain that surrounds you. So it is with us. Contemplative practices have helped me to discover the wider landscapes of my inner world, and not only locate where I truly am, despite, like Adam, the shame and worry I may feel, but also give shape and form to a more redemptive and authentic expression of myself.

There's a story of a young Hebrew boy named Samuel who spent his life in the care of an elderly priest named Eli (1 Samuel 3). The story goes that, in the dead of night, Samuel heard a voice speaking to him, calling his name in the darkness. He got out of bed and went to Eli, the man of God, saying, 'Here I am.' Eli responded (disgruntled by being woken, I'm sure) that he hadn't called the young boy and so sent him back to bed. Again, the voice speaks to Samuel and calls him forth. Samuel arises once more and wakes the old man, saying, 'Here I am. What do you want?' Again, he's sent back to his bed, but when the voice calls once more, Eli realizes something else is happening, that it is God speaking. He says to the boy, 'Go back to bed and this time when you hear the voice, say, "Speak, for your Servant is listening."'

The voice rings out just as it did before, but this time Samuel replies as he has been instructed and has a conversation with the Divine. God speaks to him of his destiny, and the course of his life is changed. There's something of Samuel's responsiveness to the voice that challenges me. Each time he heard it, in the blackness of night, he responded with 'Here I am', which says, 'I am available and I am listening.' I yearn to have the kind of attentive nature and willingness to be moved by the voice of God in my life, but when I am feeling lost, how can I say 'Here I am'? When I am feeling naked and ashamed, vulnerable and alone, how I can be courageous enough to say 'Here I am'? I spend a lot of time stumbling around in the dark with these things, but I'd love to share a simple, meditative practice I've learnt over the years that roots me in the present, acknowledges the truth of what I feel and believe and centres me towards the loving-kindness of God. It helps me, I think, to be more like the young boy Samuel, awake to the mystery.

So we do as Julian of Norwich told us when asking, 'Where do we begin?' We begin with the heart.

This is a short and simple contemplative practice that I do each day. Depending on where I am and what I'm doing, it can range from 3 minutes to 30 minutes. I do it as I go to sleep and when I wake, before meetings and hanging with friends. I have even done it on stage between songs, but its intention is always the same: to help us find ourselves and the God who is ever present, helping us to move from a feeling of being lost to being able to say of ourselves, 'Oh, there you are!'

You can do it with me right now, just following the simple stages below.

Begin by focusing on your breath for a few moments, conscious of the rise and fall in your body, aware of the inhale and exhale, the breath that sustains you, as constant as the waves crashing on countless shores every moment, the evidence of that which is faithful, constant and unchanging. Now, after feeling a sense of stillness, I simply ask myself: 'Where are you in your heart?'

This question provokes me to acknowledge my emotions and what I feel at the core and centre of my being. You may, like the Psalmist, call it 'your soul', the gut response you have to an experience. Be as authentic and honest as you can, as well as expansive in your language. Perhaps your first response is 'happy' but in lingering a little longer you realize that it's contentment or excitement you feel. Allow yourself to acknowledge the breadth and depth of that experience, fully rooting yourself in the reality of where you are in your innermost being.

Then, I go on to ask, 'Where are you in your body?'

My body is not simply a vehicle to transport my brain, nor is it the source of a 'sinful nature', but the unique craftsmanship of the Holy, an expression like no other, strong and resilient, tender and fragile, an extraordinarily complex feat of engineering and design that sustains life itself. Do you feel relaxed and comfortable in your body? Do you feel in pain or tense, perhaps? The question seeks a simple and true response that does nothing more than honour and tend to the momentary experiences we have in our bodies, locating us in the here and now. There's something quite wonderful about realizing the feeling of being dehydrated and serving yourself a cold glass of water; it demystifies the notion that there's something else going on and reconnects you to your daily dependency.

From there I ask, 'Where are you in your mind?'

In one of his letters to the early followers of Jesus, St Paul famously urged his readers to 'take every thought captive' – that is, make their thoughts obedient to Christ, higher, loftier and more enlightened to the truth. In a sense that is what this question seeks to do, to pull from the chaos of our minds a clarity by simply becoming aware of what we're thinking. Are your thoughts anxious? Are they busy? Are they perhaps set towards gratitude and expectation? Again, just to know and be aware, consciously and contemplatively, is to create the terrain around the blue dot of ourselves, acknowledging where we are and choosing to come out from our hiding.

From here you have three simple phrases to locate where you are, giving you all you need to be as truly yourself as you could be in that moment.

In my heart I am _____
In my body I am _____
In my mind I am _____

What you've done here, though simple, is profound. We spend so much of our lives moving from one place to another without fully being conscious of where we are in the midst of it. Then we have conversations, make decisions and create things, yet the whole time we're lost. It's no wonder we look back on our days wondering why we reacted the way we did to that comment or why we felt so unsatisfied with how we approached that piece of work. A contemplative practice works as a form of living water in that it enables us to become aware of where we are experiencing stagnation and staleness; we are led where so often we don't lead ourselves because of distraction and worry, lust and overthinking.

To find ourselves and be able to say 'Here I am' confronts us with our needs and our ability to give. We call out to God in a way that we wouldn't otherwise, enabling us to hear the voice we need to hear more than our own, speaking into our most impossible and overwhelming moments. I'm reminded of St Paul recounting the voice of God he heard in his pain and lostness, saying, 'My grace is sufficient for you, for my power is made perfect in weakness' (2 Corinthians 12.9).

It also makes one wonder how many disasters might have been prevented by someone confessing the fact, 'In my body I am hungry.'

And so the final part of this practice isn't so much a question as a statement of location. It is confession of where we are, however that may look, and an invitation, like Samuel, for God to meet us and speak to us as we are, not as we feel we should be.

Here I am, God. Speak, for I am listening.

From here, we rest in silence, for however long we have. Leaning into the stillness so that God might be known to us. St John of the Cross said, 'It is best to learn to silence the faculties and to cause them to be still, so that God may speak.'[8] It is as if there is something about giving up our right to have the final word that sets the stage to learn, grow and be awakened. Learning to hear God's voice takes time, trial and will remain wrapped within mystery, but we know that God is love and anyone who has seen, heard or tasted love has known God, and so we listen for the voice that is defined by loving-kindness, speaking to us as a mother tenderly speaks to her child, or as a father, provoking and challenging his beloved to be his or her truest self.

It is in practices such as these that we seek to comprehend the incomprehensible, remembering the words of Julian of Norwich:

For we are so preciously loved by God that we cannot even comprehend it. No created being can ever know how much and how sweetly and tenderly God loves them. It is only with the help of his grace that we are able to persevere in spiritual contemplation with endless wonder at his high, surpassing, immeasurable love which our Lord in his goodness has for us.[9]

My life really did change after reflecting on that Confucius quote on the shop floor that day. I began meditating every morning, I kept reading texts that awakened me to a more expansive and inclusive spirituality and set forth to live a life that was present and available, defined by loving-kindness. Ten years on, I'm still stumbling around in the dark like Samuel, still just a beginner, but I'm listening and I'm leaning in more than ever. One thing that didn't change, though, was working in retail and it didn't change for a few more years. In that time, I learnt that my creativity isn't surrendered to or suffocated by my context. To live a present life is to see that any patch of soil, when cultivated, is all you need to grow something new. So I kept writing, recording and performing any time someone offered me a show. In fact, I wrote a whole EP in my lunch breaks and in the quiet, closing hours of the shop. A few years later, I had a full-circle experience when I was notified by Superdry that one of my songs had been added to its nationwide in-store playlist – I was in the middle of a 30-date tour across the USA at the time. Ironic? Poetic? Both, I think.

The place I wanted to escape to live out my dreams was the very environment I needed to realize them.

6

A dream within a dream

Friendship is unnecessary, like philosophy, like art . . . It
has no survival value; rather it is one of those things that
gives value to survival.
(C. S. Lewis, *The Four Loves*)

One of my earliest and most vivid memories of my childhood
happened early on in our time in Pakistan. My sisters and I
watched from the windows of our home as a crowd of people
began to descend on our front garden. They sat down on the
grass, huddled in families as if they were setting up camp. We
ran and told our mother what we had seen and instinctively
she recognized these were people in need, most likely refu-
gees, travelling from the war-torn lands of Afghanistan. She
gathered us in the kitchen and began to fill our small hands
with all that we could carry: pots, pans, sacks of potatoes,
anything she could pull from the shelves of our home to help
the families feel as if they had a home. I don't remember much
else, how long they stayed, what we did next, but the feeling
of excitement and anticipation that came with serving those
families has stayed with me till this day and imprinted something on me. I think more than anything else it's the sense
that we need one another and our lives make more sense
when they are kindled together, like the wood that forms a
fire, piece upon piece, facilitating something that couldn't
happen if we were apart. It's been this energy that has given

me the vision to help to cultivate community in the soil of where I live.

Community is one of those words, like love, that gets bandied around, misused and overused to the point that it's so familiar, it's unfamiliar, and it's easy not to know exactly what someone is talking about when they use it. When I speak of community I'm speaking of lives laid down for one another, interdependent lives, leaning on one another, friendships that hold space for the length and breadth of our human experience. I'm talking about a place of belonging just because you're there, without performing or even participating, holding others long enough in their grief that your T-shirt is wetted by their tears or laughing long enough in their joy that you struggle to breathe. I'm talking about finding a cause together, a shared mission of service to others and an opportunity to do collectively what you could not have done on your own. About eating together (what is more sacred than a feast?), sharing what you have so that no one among you goes without, confronting and challenging, speaking with words of fire upon arrows of love, never letting one another live in illusion but constantly conformed to others' truest, most expressive and wildest self, whatever the cost. I'm talking about forgiving even when you can't forget and forging ways of being with one another in true unity despite disagreement because division is never an option. I'm talking about tasting heaven on earth and going through hell to get there.

Does that sound familiar?

I love what writer and theologian Henri Nouwen said: 'Community is where humility and glory touch.'[10] It so perfectly captures the cost and reward of experiencing what I've been speaking of. Over the past decade of building a community (and I say 'building' intentionally), I have experienced the highest highs and the lowest lows. I have discovered myself, my truest self, in ways that I could not have on my own and, therefore, to riff on a René Descartes' saying, 'You are, therefore I am.' Who I have become over these past ten years is in direct response to those people I have put in proximity to myself and have chosen to live a life among. I believe that community is a vessel for our creative and authentic expression, as a bucket is for living water. Although we like to think that what we create and export into the world is an independent expression of ourselves, we are formed first in the image of a relational God (Father–Son–Spirit) and second in the image of those around us. C. S. Lewis said that God works on us all through one another, as if we are the saw or the hammer in the hands of the master carpenter, carefully crafted and shaped through the lives we live together.

My wife Kara and I founded an eclectic, spiritual and creative community just after we married in 2012. It's known as Orphan No More, now with many different facets of its expression, from releasing music and touring, to serving the poor in our city and pursuing spiritual formation alongside one another. We began as four friends around a meal table, without a name or any real sense of what it might become. Every Friday night, Kara and I would cross the road to Will and Esther's apartment, where we'd spend the evening playing games and Esther and I would share songs that we had written. We'd watch films and debate theology, often at the expense of the food being cooked on time, but always end with a feast. I look back on those nights as some of the best days of my life. There was a sense, in our youth and naivety, that we were a part of something, that we had people who truly believed in us, and we felt unstoppable.

With Kara, Will and Esther's encouragement, I put out some of my music and it did pretty well, and by that I mean we could pay our rent for a few months with the earnings from it. That release put a fire in my belly to help others do the same. Esther had a ton of songs and a dream of writing an album, so we went to work on it. We spent hundreds of hours between the various apartments we lived in recording the songs however we could. There would be duvets over the door frames to make a vocal booth, and drums in the kitchen for the reverb. We'd get distracted by conversations about our desires to write songs that helped people and served to heal the wounds in our society; we'd dream of touring and imagine how incredible it would be to meet people all across the world who listened to our music and knew the lyrics to our songs. Kara and Will, far more pragmatic and strategic than us, would be the voices of reason and remind us that work was to be done and, though it took well over a year, we did it. When Esther was nine months pregnant, with her belly as big as it could grow, she performed her debut album *All Shall Be Well* at its launch in a tiny underground bar in the city.

Within a year, we had begun working with other artists in the same way, birthing a community of people who wanted to go on a journey of creativity, authenticity and service. 'Heart before Art' was the motto and our focus was on the people before the projects, the soul before the song, which looked like our recording sessions becoming counselling sessions, and, for all the chaos and naivety, we stumbled on a journey that defined a decade of our lives and will be a part of us for ever.

In 2015 Esther was diagnosed with breast cancer. Kara was with her at the hospital and I'll never forget her phone call, to let me know the result. Will came round and we spent the evening together on our living room floor, eating pizza from a place across the road. We cried, prayed and laughed, stunned by the absurdity of what we'd just discovered, but hopeful, declaring the words Esther had sung out not long before: 'All shall be well'. I won't go into much more detail about the years that followed, I don't feel it's my story to write, but throughout the turmoil of those days, watching Esther fight the sickness and seeing Will love her and their son with the courage of a warrior, I think we grew as close as any friendship this side of heaven could become.

Jesus said that there is no greater love than a life laid down for a friend and I think it's easy to view those words as being about literal death, like the one he died for us, and of course that's true, but I'm sure he was also speaking of the act of dying daily for those whom we love and seek to serve. True community is formed when you see others as having as much value, if not more, than yourself. When you lay your life down, you choose to surrender your right to be glorified for the sake of lifting someone else higher. As a practice, that can be as simple as giving up your time to serve someone's dream or need, to let another driver go before you, recognizing their destination is as important as yours to get to. When Jesus was asked, time and time again, what we must do to inherit eternal life, his response was simple but costly: ' "Love the Lord your God with all your heart and with all your soul and with all your strength and with all your mind"; and, "Love your neighbour as yourself" ' (Luke 10.27).

Jesus said that the law and all the prophets, or the entire spiritual life, can be summarized in those few words. Love. Love God, not because you have to but because you were first loved by God and the evidence of that love is hiding in plain sight. Every good and perfect thing is a gift from God, writes James the brother of Jesus; count the goodness in your life, from your relationships to your shelter, as the outpouring of affection from a kind and generous God. Look to the life of Jesus, an extravagant display of mercy and compassion, ultimately leading to a torturous death, displaying the love and tenderness God feels towards you. Now, love your neighbour as you love yourself. When Jesus was asked by a scholar trying to catch him out, 'Who is my neighbour?', he went on to tell the story of a man who was beaten and robbed on his way to the city (Luke 10.25–37). Some religious leaders walked past the man, crossing the road in disgust and avoidance, and thus it wasn't until a Samaritan man, hated by the Jews on the basis of his race, came by that the man was saved. The Samaritan bandaged him up, gave him all he had and even paid for his recovery at an inn. Jesus asked the man, 'Who was the one who acted as a neighbour to the man in need?' and the scholar replied, 'The one who showed mercy.' 'Go and do likewise,' said Jesus.

There was a time when Kara and I lived on the ground floor of a block of flats and we had the loudest couple living upstairs.

They'd make so much noise with everything they did – we could hear them cooking, listening to music, talking and everything in-between. They'd keep us up at all hours and we began to get increasingly frustrated with them. Having been challenged by the way Jesus taught us to be a neighbour, we prayed one night that we could have more compassion towards them and an opportunity to serve them and, I kid you not, within minutes of praying that prayer, just after midnight, there was a knock at the door. There stood the woman who lived upstairs. She told me that she and her partner, who was shirtless, cowering behind her, had been locked out of their flat and could I call the locksmith for them. We invited them in, I gave him some Orphan No More merch to wear and we went into the living room. I called a locksmith and, with my hand over the phone, told them he'd come out, but at this time of night it would cost £200. They both agreed that was too much so I happily tried again. The next bloke said that he'd do it for less, but his price was the lowest we'd get at what was now about 1 a.m. I told them he'd do it for £100. They glanced at each other nervously and then looked back at me, mouthing the words 'That's too much'. So I put down the phone and said, 'Looks like we're having a sleepover.' We got them set up on the airbed and the next morning we lingered over some coffee, got to know one another and then they went on their way to find a locksmith.

Kara and I burst out laughing when they left. The people we wanted to be more compassionate towards were sleeping in our spare room, within moments of praying that prayer, and instantaneously the frustration simmered down and, I have to say, the noise did as well.

We create a neighbour at the other end of our compassion and an enemy at the end of our judgement and fear.

Living in a community with others costs you, and that's the point. Some things are expensive for a good reason. Some things cost you who you don't want to be and, for us, community is one of those things. Community costs you your pride. When you live in close proximity to others, involving them in your life, inviting them to speak into your decision-making, celebrating your wins and lamenting your losses with them, you can only have an artificial sense of yourself for so long before someone reminds you of who you truly are. Humbling? Oh yes. Every time, but, like wood in the hands of a skilled craftsman, it shapes your life into the work of art it was always meant to be.

When I look back at my life, I can see the opportunities I missed out on for the sake of not going about it alone but bringing more people with me along the way. You can't go as fast with others as you would on your own, you have to consult and consider the feelings and perspectives they carry. Sometimes it's infuriating but, honestly, it costs me the sharp edges of my character that I don't want to have. I got signed with a label in Nashville a few years ago and, as soon as the deal went through, I felt a phrase come to mind: 'The doors that open for you lead to rooms that are destined for others.' What it meant for me was that my life isn't the main event and there's room at the table for everyone if someone's willing to share their plate and make room for a chair, as countless others have done for me. The next time I went to Nashville a couple from our community came with us, the time after that a few more and the last time we went there were so many artists from the UK touching down, we got called the 'British Invasion'. I watched as they took sessions and meetings with people introduced to me by the label, and honestly sighed with relief knowing that it wasn't just me who had walked through that open door.

I'm not saying all this to sound great. I've been selfish just as much as I've been sacrificial and I've been prideful far more than humble, but I know that my life has been marked by the presence of others and I am so grateful for it.

The last time we saw Esther was when Kara and I flew out to visit her in hospital. She had been in a special cancer treatment facility in the States. We shared some precious moments at her bedside; I made her a playlist of songs that she wanted to have blaring out in her sterile hospital room. She requested one that we had written but not released, so we recorded it as soon as we got home. It wasn't long after we got back to England that Esther passed away, her husband and parents at her side and hundreds (if not thousands) around the world leaning in, praying for her, enamoured by the story of a young woman who had faced such suffering and heart-break, yet remained so full of true and sober joy, faith and hope throughout.

A few weeks later, Will asked if I'd lead the service in cele-bration of her life and it was and will forever be one of the great honours of my life, standing up there in front of friends, family and others who, having been so influenced by Esther's story, had travelled from far and wide to take part in the service.

I remember the night before feeling at a loss for how to end the time together. Nothing could tie a nice neat bow on the events that led to that day, not simply because of the pain and confusion but also because no bow, however pretty, could be worthy of adorning a story that only deserved a crown.

As the night drew to a close and with my whisky glass empty, I sighed and submitted to the night, accepting I may have to start the service unsure of how it would end, trusting that somehow I'd find my footing. As I slowly lifted myself out of the garden chair, my eyes red and heavy, my lungs filled with the warm peaty aroma of my single malt companion, a text from a friend sounded on my phone. It simply read, 'I think this might help.'

What it contained was a poem usually ascribed to Henry Van Dyke, an American author and clergyman. As I read it, salty tears began to stream down my cheeks and a hopeful sob began to rise from my gut.

I read this poem at the closing of Esther's funeral and my dad told me he read it to my grandfather as he fell into that great and inevitable slumber, the sleep that awaits us all as our days draw to their end.

I am standing upon the seashore.
A ship at my side spreads her white
sails to the morning breeze and starts for the blue ocean.

She is an object of beauty and strength.
I stand and watch her until at length

she hangs like a speck of white cloud
just where the sea and sky come
to mingle with each other.

Then, someone at my side says,
'There, she is gone!'

'Gone where?'
Gone from my sight. That is all.
She is just as large in mast and hull
and spar as she was when she left my side
and she is just as able to bear her
load of living freight to her destined port.
Her diminished size is in me, not in her.

And just at the moment when someone
at my side says, 'There, she is gone!'
There are other eyes watching her coming,
and other voices ready to take up the glad shout,
'Here she comes!'

The winter after Esther passed away, I went walking with Will and our friend Jon. It was Will's thirtieth birthday, so we set some time aside to spend together in our grief and bewilderment, celebrating this incredible man who had already suffered so deeply and loved so courageously at such a young age. While walking through the rugged beauty of the Brecon Beacons, I was reflecting on the profound impact of our friendship and my mind drifted to the opening scene in Christopher Nolan's (incredible) film *Inception*. There's a profound piece of dialogue that has helped me to process loss and purpose within friendship since that day. Cobb, played by Leonardo DiCaprio, has descended deep into the dream world, to find and rescue his friend Saito, who by now has grown into an old man, aged by illusion and weary in the slumber of escape.

> COBB: I've come back for you . . . to remind you of something. Something you once knew, that this world is not real.
> SAITO: To convince me to honor our arrangement.
> COBB: To take a leap of faith, yes. Come back . . . so we can be young men together again. Come back with me . . .

At the opening of this chapter, I described community as heaven on earth and I mean that, truly. To experience friendship is to experience eternity here and now, which is why it's most painful when we lose someone who reminded us of who we truly are and how special it is to be here. Community, in this lifetime, in this broken, beaten-up but breathtakingly beautiful world, is the art of keeping one another awake. The process of reminding one another that there is a bigger and better story at work, a redemptive and hopeful narrative, whose author isn't fear.

We keep one another from falling asleep in the pain, in the desire to be numbed and, as a result, walk away from wonder and expectation. We are here to remind one another of something we once knew: a joy before it was stolen by cynicism and disappointment, a hope before we ever felt it deferred, love without fear or reservation. We celebrate one another in a world built on competition and comparison, we forgive one another when others seek revenge and rejection, we lay down our lives while others hold on to theirs with the white-knuckled grip of control.

We remind one another that we will be young friends together again.

RECLAIM

7

The light in the tunnel

A guilty conscience needs to confess. A work of art is a confession.
(Albert Camus, *Notebooks*)

When lockdown came into full force during the spring of 2020, I found myself in a new and unique position. For the first time in months, I had nowhere to be. No events, tours or engagements that meant I'd be packing my bags and skipping town. A few really special things came of that: I was home for the entirety of my wife's final few months of pregnancy; I discovered some new hobbies and interests; I read more; and every Friday, around 3 p.m., I would meet my two best mates for a walk to close off the week. Each week, one of us would grab a round of beverages and we'd walk for an hour or two, catching up and generally enjoying the rare opportunity just to be together. Spontaneously, one week we started a new rhythm during our time together: confession.

Now, I know that can sound like a heavy word with stuffy religious connotations, one that may conjure images of protagonists of films sitting in a dark confession box and admitting unwanted thoughts or feelings to a cold and distant priest. I went to a Catholic school and remember the condemning language that surrounded this ancient practice – I wanted nothing to do with it. The truth is, though, as I've grown older I've come to realize how deeply we all need to express that which seems inexpressible. Confession, as a spiritual practice, dates back thousands of years. In fact Jesus' own brother James wrote to the early Church with this provocation: 'Therefore, confess your sins to one another [your false steps, your offences], and pray for one another, that you may be healed and restored' (James 5.16, AMP).

Our confession brings healing?

Absolutely.

I've seen it with my own eyes, more times than I can count. It doesn't take long for us to get tangled up inside. The weight of our own shame and self-condemnation is frankly too heavy to bear. I remember sitting with a friend whose body was contorted under the burden he bore. He had asked to see me, though he hadn't gone into any detail why. When I saw him, I was taken aback – his eyes were darkened, his shoulders seemed to have collapsed, too heavy to hold up, and his face stared blankly towards the floor. This was a man with much hidden and there was only one way out. I spoke to him gently: 'Whatever it is you need to tell me, I won't be shocked.'

Most often we struggle to share what is deepest within us because we have believed the lie that we're the only one capable of thinking or doing such things. The horror of our own thoughts and actions begins to haunt us and convince us that if anyone should ever find out, we'd surely be abandoned, looked upon with repulsion and disgust.

With tears streaming down his cheeks, he began to sob. There's something about a grown man weeping that levels you. This was a cry of anguish, remorse and regret. My heart broke for him. Without knowing what he was going to say, I knew he needed healing, nothing else mattered. I recounted those ancient words, centuries old, 'Confess your sins, that you may be healed.'

Between his sobs and awkward glances around the room, he told me he had been having an affair, that he had fallen for a colleague and, though he had ended it, hadn't yet told his wife. The release that came with the words spilling from his lips was magnificent. He sat back on the sofa and sighed deeply, as if his exhaustion had just caught up with him. Whimpers still bounced around the room but he was calmer and slightly more composed.

I asked him to look at me because if there's one way to banish shame, it's through the gaze of another human being. Eye contact simply says, 'I see you' and sometimes that is all we need to know, that we're not alone in this world. Shame has played a nefarious role in the human story since the beginning. The Hebrew creation poem speaks of a time when man and woman walked with God in the cool of the day; they were friends, intimate and connected. One day, God came looking for them, anticipating their daily stroll, but they were nowhere to be found. Hiding behind the trees, aware of their stark nakedness, they called out to him. The story tells us that, moments before, they had been caught in a web of lies, seduced by the voice of a tempter; they abandoned the simplicity they enjoyed with God for the illusive, ego-driven desires within.

When they realized that they'd been conned and fallen from the path of peace they walked on, they felt afraid, so they hid, fearfully anticipating the arrival of the God they knew so well. The poetry is so poignant because it speaks to a reality we can all testify to be true. Shame makes us aware of ourselves in a way that only causes us to hide. It is the sense not that we have *done* something wrong but that inherently we *are* something wrong. Our naked bodies become a battleground of self-disgust and our inner universe is submerged into chaos. We hide to protect ourselves and, if we're truly honest, to protect others from who we now believe ourselves to be. Our hiding is a form of control, a manipulative, cohesive attempt to find pseudo freedom in the arms of our captor. Shame is Stockholm syndrome at its most perennial and perverse. There is only one way out. As captors and captives, we cannot free ourselves. If God had not returned to the garden that day, perhaps humanity would never have broken free from the fear, shame, control cycle that bound us. For it is only in confession, bearing our nakedness before another, that we can rediscover our original goodness and inherent worth.

I thanked him for telling me, that I couldn't imagine how hard it was to share and then I declared the words Julian of Norwich professed in her sickness: 'All shall be well.'

That confession was the beginning of a long and difficult journey, but set him on to a path that led him into an inner reformation and an incredible reconciliation with his wife. After months of counselling and therapy, together and apart, they have newfound love, respect and trust for each other.

I told him to look into my eyes after his confession because I knew the power of that experience for myself. A few years ago, my wife and I had got into a massive amount of debt. We were living on very little money, and the accessibility of credit cards and overdrafts seemed like a saving grace when bills were missed and the rent was overdue again. On top of that, we were pursuing the creative path, writing and releasing music, building a record label and playing shows up and down the country, none of which paid much at all. Things spiralled and got out of control. I kept some of it from Kara because I was convinced that a payout was coming which would balance everything out and, instead of bringing it into a tangled web of uncertainty and lack, I could present her with a solution and financial security.

The problem was, that day didn't come but the bills did, so things got worse and worse. I remember it with piercing clarity, the moment I got a call from the debt collector, announcing that I was out of time and if I didn't pay what I owed, the bailiffs were coming. We were at a friend's party and for the rest of the day I sat with a knot in my stomach, unable to engage with anyone, like a rabbit chased by the dogs, cornered in the woods with nowhere left to run, nowhere left to hide. I was out of options.

When we got home, I told Kara, not out of courage or conviction but helplessness. It was like throwing myself off a diving board I wasn't brave enough to intentionally jump from. She was in the kitchen washing up, so with her back turned me I started to let it all spill out. I couldn't look at her, so kept my eyes locked on the floor. I hated that I did this to us. As soon as I finished my monologue of mortification, she asked me to look at her. I remember light in her eyes and a smile across her face, as if I had just told her the best news. She simply said, 'I love you and everything is going to be OK.' I crumpled into her arms. The burden I had carried in isolation had been lifted and, like a splash of cold water on my face in the morning, I felt awake for the first time in a while. Again, it was a long road ahead, one that we're still treading, but I'm not walking it alone.

We have all, in one way or another, caused harm, if not to someone else then to ourselves. We have disturbed the shalom within and what is hidden cannot be healed.

Confession is a deeply creative act because it bypasses the eloquence of our ego, the showmanship of our self-righteousness and gives voice to the tortured artist who is our truest self. The most formidable art is confessional. I remember digesting (what is one of my top five albums of all time) Kanye West's *Late Registration* album and feeling an instant connection with his song 'Addiction'. He asks the question why supposedly bad things make him feel good and wrestles, as St Paul did 2,000 years before, with the notion of doing the very thing that he doesn't want to do while not doing the very thing he does want to.

Or you might have seen Rembrandt's self-portrait, one the most valued and respected pieces of his prolific career. His sunken eyes and weathered skin tell the story of a man who wrestled with many demons, yet had turned away from the shallow, egocentric passions of his younger years, displaying his true embattled but solemnly peaceful self in what I'd like to call a visual confession.

Perhaps you've read the inescapable honesty in Mary Oliver's poem 'The Swimming Lesson', in which she laments the experience of falling into and rising above the water not as liberation and grace but as a foretelling of the struggle and desire to belong in her body and a place.

When you confess your pain, your limitations, wrongdoing or the shame you feel, like clay in the hands of a potter you begin the process of making something new, something of true beauty from the dirt itself. Confession brings the form our flow needs to travel. There's something in you that needs to be out here and it might begin as an ugly cry of remorse or a scribbled letter you'll never send. It might be the acknowledgement of a dream that died, for which you never gave yourself space to grieve, or the envy you feel towards another.

On our walks each week, we gave form to the flow and released it into a space that was safe, un-shockable and capable of reminding us who we truly are. We'd take turns confessing whatever needed to find its way out. Once we had shared, the other two would simply say, 'We absolve you', acting as priests to one another, sipping our beers, declaring pardon and release from the heavy burden of guilt we had carried.

We'd time our conversation so our confessions began as we walked through the darkness of an old, decommissioned train tunnel. As our words rang out, echoing against the brick walls, we'd have the constant glimmer of light leading us onwards. It spoke to me of the inevitable grace that awaits those who walk into the darkness of their shadowlands, the mercy that rises each morning with our faithful sun, the forgiveness that reorders our chaotic world and heals our wounded selves.

8

Lord, have mercy

Only the man who has had to face despair is really convinced that he needs mercy. Those who do not want mercy never seek it. It is better to find God on the threshold of despair than to risk our lives in a complacency that has never felt the need of forgiveness. A life that is without problems may literally be more hopeless than one that always verges on despair.
(Thomas Merton, *No Man is an Island*)

I was 15 and up to no good. I woke up in the garden, as the sun began to rise, with my head pounding and my body shivering. I craved nothing more than a warm shower and hot cup of tea, so I decided to make the pilgrimage home. I figured walking back shouldn't take more than an hour and it was only just morning. As I walked, my mind drifted to the night before, to how I had ended up here.

There had been rumours of a party happening that Friday night. Someone's parents were away, which meant, among other things, that it would be a welcome change from the cold streets where we'd drink our cheap cider that we'd buy with our fake IDs. I'd known this was going to be an all-nighter so I started working on the logistics. I told my mum that I was staying at my friend's house; he told his mum the same and, although neither of us relished lying to our mothers, we needed a story that would help us to escape our curfews.

I stumbled home in the hazy blue light of dawn, the roads empty and the world as quiet as it had ever been. A mile or so into my journey I noticed a car coming my way, its dipped beams creating a path of light through the sea of morning mist. I wondered what someone was up to so early in the day and then my mind drifted to other things. It wasn't until the car inched closer that it caught my attention once again. I recognized it. The long body of a red Volvo estate came into view and before I could fully process its familiarity, I saw my mum's face in the driving seat, eyes locked upon me as the car drifted past me, swiftly swallowed into the sea of mist.

I stopped walking.

What were the chances?

The final mile home was the longest journey I had ever travelled. With a knot tightening in my stomach and my heart throbbing in my chest, I tried to think up excuses that would make any kind of sense. My mind was blank. There's nothing like the shame that comes from getting caught while doing what you knew was wrong in the first place. Most of my teenage years were spent trying to find who I was in a sea of possibilities. I drank, did drugs and other regrettable things in a hopeless attempt to feel at home within myself. I had spent most of my life moving around and there's a certain complexity that comes with not knowing where you come from. It gives you the chance to reinvent yourself, but at the expense of integration. Seeing my mum's face that morning confronted me with the reality of my inward division. I had never felt more lost.

I had read the Bible most days of my young life and, despite the reckless choices that I was making at the time, my spiritual compass stayed set towards its magnetic north. In times of distress, my mind would wander back to familiar passages that brought comfort and solace, as well the sting of a holy rebuke. I felt like the lost son in one of Jesus' stories. The boy who left home, taking his share of an inheritance that was premature. He squandered it all, spending it on fast living and hedonistic choices until it ran out, which it always does. When he found himself broke and starving, he collapsed into the lowest of all vocations – a pig feeder on a farm. As he brought food to the swine, an animal considered to be impure, he collapsed on his knees under the weight of his own hunger and desperation and began to eat with them. Jesus is telling the story of a man who literarily can't get any lower. It's at that moment he decided to go home, at breaking point, the bottom of the barrel, at land's end. As he crawled home, he began to prepare a speech for his father – one of remorse and regret, just as I was doing. He resolved that he'd tell his father he wasn't coming back as a son but as a servant, no longer worthy to be considered family. We've all done that. The inner monologue we perform is an attempt to redefine our place in the world, a response to our own self-disgust and failure. There was a tradition at that time where the people of the town, when seeing a wayward son returning, would run to meet him and smash a clay pot at his feet, a representation of the broken trust between them and an announcement of the shame he now carried. So it's no small detail when Jesus added this line in his story: 'While he was a long way off, his father saw him and was filled with compassion for him; he ran to meet his son, threw his arms round him and kissed him' (Luke 15.20).

Not caring about the humiliation of running, as an older, patriarchal figure, the father sprints towards his tormented child, wrapping him in his arms of compassion and grace before the condemning traditional act can take place. Jesus, as always, is speaking to us of a much deeper and transcendent truth. If you decide to come home, back to your true and original self, no matter where you have been, how long you've been there and what you've been doing, you will be met by the unrestricted and unending love of God.

Before the son can even utter his speech, his father has clothed him in new robes, restored him to his place in the family and ordered a feast to take place that very night, in celebration of his return. The story doesn't end there, but that's for another book.

I climbed on to my bed when I got home and sobbed. It was probably as much the hangover and tiredness I felt as anything else, but I did have an acute awareness of my lostness. There's only so long that you can go on fighting a war within yourself. I had spent that year making some pretty damaging choices, decisions that would have an impact on me and others for years to come. I had forsaken many of the values I once held dear and felt that I didn't know who I was any more. Richard Rohr says, 'You can't heal something with the same consciousness that caused it' and in my own simplistic way, I think I knew that truth back then. Lying on my bed alone, stinking of cheap liquor and weed, I uttered a phrase that was familiar to me but I didn't fully understand: 'Lord, have mercy.'

I had heard people say those words before, but it's taken me more than a decade to fully appreciate the depth and life-changing impact of that sacred, ancient phrase. What I've realized over the years is that asking for mercy is seeking a change to the way you see. You can't change a problem with the same consciousness that caused it and so, like the wayward son, there comes a point when we have to accept that it's time to turn around; the way we're living isn't producing living water but a stale and stagnated pond that breeds disease for the soul. That's actually where the word 'repentance' comes from. I always associated it with the Bible bashing, fire-and-brimstone preaching, shouty men on the side of the road, with their apocalyptic messages ringing out, 'Repent, for the end is near.' I'm not knocking them, do your thing, bruv, but the true meaning of those words runs a lot deeper than what could be conveyed in that way. It comes from the Greek word *metanoia*, meaning beyond thought, with *meta* meaning 'after' or 'beyond' (as in the word 'metaphysics') and *nous* meaning 'mind'. To repent is to change the way you think, to turn around and, as a result, see the world and yourself renewed and through a new lens.

Our receiving or giving of mercy leads us into an experience of repentance, for it removes us from the cycle of retribution that we've been taught to pursue. To be merciful is to show compassion and forgiveness to someone whom you have the power to punish. In Jesus' story of the prodigal son, we see just that. The father had every right to persecute his boy but chose to meet him with affection instead of an affliction. Jesus is telling us that this is what God is like. Ultimate reality. It's as if he's saying that the greatest power in all the universe, who has the sovereignty and potency to punish, has chosen not to.

The source of all living things, in whom we live and move and have our being, is, in fact, the place where we always hoped to be – the wide-open spaces of grace and mercy.

When you give and receive forgiveness, you bear witness to the true power of love.

As Jesus hung on the splintered cross, with nine-inch nails penetrating his wrists and feet, with a crown of thorns piercing through to his skull, with his flesh hanging off his body, limp with exhaustion and pain, he uttered these words: 'Father, forgive them, for they do not know what they are doing' (Luke 23.34)

Jesus wasn't just forgiving the soldiers who tortured him but also every torturous act that we have afflicted upon one another and, indeed, ourselves. The death of Jesus revealed what we are capable of as humans, our violence and bloodlust, but also his capacity to show mercy towards those who inflicted violence on him. Receiving mercy releases mercy, and so to acknowledge that God has extended his grace and forgiveness towards you not only sets you free from the cyclical misery of shame but also empowers you to do the same for others. Forgiveness reorders our world and releases humanity from its bondage.

Forgiveness isn't fair; no one ever deserves it – that's the point. It's a gift that you can't earn, unlike responsibility or trust. Forgiveness is freely given but it's expensive. It will cost you your desire for justice. It will cost you the power you feel by wielding resentment over someone, and sometimes, when you've been greatly hurt by another, that power can feel good.

But it will also cost you who you don't want to be. It will cost you to become someone who's tormented inside, someone who sees the face of the perpetrator on everybody else because you never released them. Unforgiveness locks the person who hurt you in a jail cell. The only problem is, you're locked in there with that person. There is no version of our lives without suffering, without being hard done by and hurt by others; forgiveness empowers us to become someone who is truly free within it.

You may know the story of Eva Kor. She was arrested with her family by the Nazis in 1944. Upon arriving at Auschwitz, soldiers pried apart her tiny fingers, clasped around her mother, and kidnapped her along with her twin sister Miriam. They became the subjects of horrific experiments at the merciless hands of Dr Josef Mengele. They were 10 years old. Eva fought for survival, battling against the concoctions injected into her body, her singular reason for survival being to prevent the doctors from killing her sister as well. The twins made it through the trauma of Auschwitz only to find that their home was empty and learn everyone else in their family had been murdered.

Years later, Eva's beloved twin sister Miriam passed away, her body having still been affected by the experiments of the concentration camp. Eva fell into the trenches of pain and sorrow, having lost the only remaining survivor of her family. In 1984, as an attempt to find healing for her soul and traumatic past, she took the extraordinary step of contacting a Nazi doctor, Hans Münch. Hans Münch had been stationed outside the gas chambers at Auschwitz, where he told Eva how he would sign the death certificates not with names and identities but as mass body counts on the day. Eva saw the remorse and regret that he carried and 'the nightmare he lived every day'. She asked him to join her on a trip to Auschwitz, where they would sign a declaration refuting the lies of those who denied that the Holocaust took place. Ten months later, in an astonishing display of mercy, Eva penned a letter of forgiveness to Münch, as a survivor of the camp, giving him the undeserving gift of grace. She said that she knew it changed his life, but what she discovered for herself was astounding: she had a power no one could give or take away, the power of forgiveness. She went on to forgive Mengele, the merciless doctor who put her and Miriam through hell, and spoke of it, saying:

> Though it wasn't easy, I finally felt free, a huge weight had been lifted from upon me. Who decided that I as a victim should live angry, helpless and hopeless? I refuse it. You can never change what happened in the past but how you react. My sister and I were made into human guinea pigs and my entire family was murdered but I have the power to forgive and so do you.[11]

Eva's story compels us to live, to truly and fully live. She refused to allow the water in her soul to grow stagnant and found form for its flow in the most staggering way.

Mercy is one of the most creative expressions we carry, for it brings forth new life in the most desolate lands. I have seen a rose grow in concrete, beauty breaking through the hardened shell of a calloused heart when someone confesses the words of forgiveness, both in receiving it and giving it away.

Try it now. Take a deep breath in and, on the exhale, simply utter the words, 'Lord, have mercy.' Perhaps like Eva or Jesus you are saying this towards another, someone who has done you wrong, caused you harm and poured shame on you. Perhaps, like me, you are confessing these words for your own soul, as a return home to love and grace and peace.

I want to close this chapter with a story that puts fire in my belly. I love reading it and talking about it because it calls out courage from within and empowers me to declare my desires, manifest my intentions and speaks to me about the power of seeking mercy, of what can happen when we throw off the cloak of our shame in pursuit of our liberation.

The story goes that Jesus was leaving the city of Jericho with a massive crowd around him. He had a growing following – that's what happens when you're the voice of the people and you rage against the machine. He was healing the sick, casting out demons and making religious people squirm with his un-dignified displays of love and acceptance. There was a blind man sitting on the side of the road begging (it would have been a commonplace to do that), just outside the city where people would be passing by. The blind man realized that it was Jesus who was approaching, so he began to cry out in a loud voice: 'Jesus, Son of David, have mercy on me!' (Luke 18.38).

His choice of words is interesting because he acknowledged Jesus' place in the line of kings. Naming him as the son of David spoke of his royal identity, something that most people missed. Anyway, you can imagine how loud he had to scream to try to be heard over the throng of people. His voice is hoarse and stretched; struggling to break through the clamour and chaos, he cries out. People start to tell him to shut up, they rebuke him, even the men who are friends of Jesus tell the blind man to be silent. What does he do in response? The story says that he cried out all the more: 'Son of David, have mercy on me!'

Though the crowds mocked and rebuked him, Jesus stops walking and says, 'Bring him to me.' Absolutely freaking epic. The blind man gets up and we are told that he throws off his coat. This is important because, for a blind man in the first century, his coat identified him by his ailment. They would paint a mark on their outer garment so people in the busy market streets wouldn't knock them down. It was as if he knew that where he was going meant he wouldn't need it any longer.

The blind man stands in front of Jesus, this leader of a new movement, this famous revolutionary bringing hope to the hopeless and dignity to the scorned. Jesus simply asks him, 'What do you want me to do for you?'

Staggering.

Isn't it obvious? He's blind – surely you would know that he wants to see. It is as though Jesus is confronting us with a God who doesn't define us the way others do, who doesn't see our weakness or suffering as the most obvious thing about us. He doesn't view us as a victim and so his question is filled with dignity and genuine curiosity. It also speaks to me of the space the Divine gives to us to declare our deepest desires.

Who taught you that what you long for is wrong? Who said you must sacrifice your dreams for the fulfilment of someone else's? Forgive them, they knew not what they did because Jesus reveals the question that God is asking each one of us: what do you want me to do for you? If our answer is buried beneath the weight of false humility and self-martyrdom, what hope can we have of experiencing the living water that runs within us when a desire is fulfilled. I have found that the most refreshing, revitalizing and hydrating people to be around are those who have, despite mockery and rejection, disappointment and affliction, pursued the desires in their heart with humility and hopefulness. Though hope deferred makes the heart grow sick, a desire fulfilled is like a tree of life. Trees of life are the ones that provide fruit for the hungry, shade for the weary and branches for the children to play on.

'I want to see,' says the blind man, and immediately he receives his sight.

What began as a cry for mercy ended with the miracle of seeing. Sometimes we need to fall on our knees in desperation and scream into the chaos, recognizing our confession as the expression that could lead to a most unlikely resurrection.

9

I'm not creative

Now the earth was formless and empty, darkness was over the surface of the deep, and the Spirit of God was hovering over the waters. And God said, 'Let there be light,' and there was light.
(Genesis 1.2–3)

Every culture has a different account of how things came to be, of how life originated and how our universe, for all we know of it, was conceived. Greek mythology begins with chaos, a void of nothingness from which emerged the earth and divine beings whose epic narratives of war and love have lived on to this day. In ancient Mesopotamia, stories were kindled of the gods and their beloved union that gave birth to sky and sea. One of the Hindu stories features the god Brahma, who first creates, by thought alone, the waters. He buries a seed beneath the deep, which grows into a golden egg, from which he is born, then splits the egg to form two halves, heaven and earth. I wonder if you've heard of P'an Ku, the Chinese deity who, like Brahma, was born within a cosmic egg, growing tall, pushing the shell apart to form the sky and earth? After 18,000 years of holding these mighty shell pillars in tension, he collapses into pieces. His limbs become the mountains, his blood the rivers, his breath the wind and his voice the thunder. His two eyes are the sun and the moon, and the parasites on his body are humankind (what a compliment!).

Perhaps you've read *A Brief History of Time* and agree with the great mind of Stephen Hawking, who mused elsewhere:

> I believe the simplest explanation is, there is no God. No one created the universe and no one directs our fate. This leads me to a profound realisation that there probably is no heaven and no afterlife either. We have this one life to appreciate the grand design of the universe and for that, I am extremely grateful.[12]

Of course, there is the ancient Hebrew story with which we are more familiar, that God, the uncreated one, spoke all that is into being, recorded in the poetic verses of Genesis.

Whatever you believe, however literal or metaphorical, whether rooted in science or spiritual tradition, we want to know where this all began; we're intrigued, if not obsessed, with comprehending how such beauty and complexity could have been fashioned from nothing at all. I think part of our curiosity about the cosmic creation story comes from the innate compulsion within us all to create something new of our own. The story of humanity is one of creative survival, from building the first fire to engineering the first bridge, we use this innovative, evolutionary instinct not just to extend our lifetime but also to enrich it. You're reading this book upon pages with ink thanks to Johannes Gutenberg, a political exile in Germany who engineered the printing press machine in the fourteenth century. There's the light bulb above your head thanks to Humphry Davy, an inventor from Cornwall who connected wires to a battery and a piece of carbon, which in turn caused the carbon to glow, producing light. I'm sitting writing these words with my laptop on a table. The idea of a table was believed to have been conceived thousands of years back by the ancient Egyptians, who adorned their tombs with tables laden with food for the deceased to feast upon in the afterlife.

Everything comes from nothing and I see that every day among the people around me. I work with designers, photographers, musicians and dancers regularly, but the most innovative person in my team is my accountant, who, as in the Greek story of creation, turns the chaos I give him into order. My wife is a counsellor and her work is to hold space for people in all they feel and have experienced and, over time, with care she helps to transform the pain, confusion and judgement they feel towards themselves and others into peace, forgiveness and harmony. There is a woman who works at the railway station where I live and I've seen her and spoken to her more times than I can count during my decade of train travel. Even when I've been frustrated and flustered, rushing for a train at the crack of dawn, she has never ceased to be the kindest and gentlest woman I've ever met. She does her job with passion and fervour and creates an atmosphere of holy grace from within that ticket booth. My mum was a nurse for a long time and then stopped so she could bring us up, her four kids. Despite the number of times we moved, she made our home feel like a place where we were truly safe and could express ourselves, and brought our family together with traditions and rituals that have shaped the man I am today.

My friend Josh is a baker (among other things) and, like a scientist, with incredible attention to detail, he combines ingredients that on their own seem to serve little purpose but when mixed with others make the most delicious cinnamon twists. My brother-in-law is a building surveyor and when he's not designing and project managing in an office, he's on-site, helping the construction, building the facilities that enable our industries. My friend Martha helps bewildered new parents to navigate how to train their babies to sleep through the night, creating space for quality time and sleep in those tiresome seasons. My friend Will is a consultant and, with research and the most mind-boggling spreadsheets, he helps businesses to expand and flourish. My other brother-in-law worked as a porter in a hospital during the pandemic. He told us how honoured he felt, leading people with dignity and sorrow on their final passage through the hospital hallways. My dad is a doctor, who spends most of his life working with people who are caught in the horrors of addiction, helping them with medicine and care to keep on living, one day at a time. My friend Deborah is an athlete. She represented Great Britain in the Olympics in 2020 and, with devotion and discipline to her craft, she inspires us to realize what the human body is capable of, with power and grace.

It seems to me that one thing we're all unable to do is to cease creating. I say all that to disrupt the notion that you may or may not be 'creative'. Unfortunately, over the past 100 years (with the birth of mass marketing), we've come to believe a shallow definition of creativity, embedded in our societies by huge corporations with nothing but profit-driven agendas. We've been sold the notion that being creative is just another way of getting ahead, becoming more employable, a means of gaining followers, money and esteem, and so we judge our ability to create by whether the craft we pursue yields that kind of harvest. We plaster terms like 'a creative individual' on our résumés and networking profiles, we wear it like a badge of honour that separates the wheat from the chaff, not realizing how ridiculous it is to do so.

The question isn't are we or are we not creative, the question is what do we do with our creativity? We've believed the lie so completely that I can't tell you how many people have told me that they are 'just not the creative type'. I respond with 'What do you mean? Are you telling me that someone else dressed you, fed you and decided all your actions for the day? And if not, when does your creativity begin and end? Which movement begins the creative expression you're telling me that you're incapable of?' More often than not, they are simply comparing what they have produced with their time and ability in the context of, or in comparison to, mine or someone else's, and in the process nullified their contributions.

To create is to bring something into existence that wasn't there before – something we all do, every day, instinctively. It's the way we respond to a hurtful comment with grace and create a redemptive rather than reactionary end; it's the way we make eye contact and smile at the shopkeeper, dignifying an interaction with a fellow human rather than it being simply a transaction. It's the way we care for our children, choosing to create an environment where they feel free to express themselves, and it's the way we love and care for our bodies and souls. Not only are we subdued in our expression when believing we're not creative but I also think this distracts us from a more provocative and meaningful question: what did you do with your creativity? To be told that I'm creative is as much a compliment as being told I am capable of feeding and dressing myself. To be told I am intentional with my creativity is far more of a compliment. To be intentional is to place value and care, attention and honour on something and someone.

After Jesus heals the blind man, the very same disciples who mocked him and rebuked him, telling him to be silent, are reported as dancing and singing in the streets, proclaiming the good news of all that they have seen Jesus do before them. Some proud and pious men tell Jesus to silence his followers and he responds by saying, 'If I tell them to be silent, the very rocks beneath their feet will cry out' (Luke 19.40, my paraphrase).

It's as if he's saying that the whole order of creation is set towards gratitude, that we were all designed with an innate ability to bring form and expression to what we experience, and if something as lifeless as a stone could do it, how could you not?

If creativity (the ability to create something from nothing) is more of an instinct for the human than it is a gift or talent, reserved for the few, and if our definition of what it means to be successfully creative is rooted more in an agenda driven by capitalism to generate wealth than it is the organic expression of our souls, then what is it that separates those who seem to harness their creativity in a way others do not? I would suggest we look no further than to the natural cycles of creation for our answer.

This brings me to talk about one of my favourite subjects of all: salmon. The short life of salmon (averaging about four years) is brutal but filled with life lessons. Salmon spend most of their lives making the death-defying pilgrimage back upstream, towards the river bed where they were born. With their scaled bodies bashed against the rocks, escaping the claws and jaws of grizzlies and other predators, they defy the odds and lay their eggs, birthing the next generation. There is this evolutionary instinct within salmon to swim home, to make the long journey back to where it all began, because they know, somewhere deep in their salmon souls, that it's the best place to start again. Once they've reached their destination and spawn, exhausted and fulfilled, they pass away, to the great ocean in the sky, reunited with the salmon saints of old.

Of course, the metaphor breaks down, but I think that there's something to learn from salmon. It fascinates me how the salmon choose to swim upstream to perform the great creative act they are destined for. They could simply spawn in the gentle tide of the ocean, but instead they risk their lives, fighting against the white water as they swim.

The question isn't do you have the capacity to create, the question is do you have the courage?

Courage isn't about showing up looking like Superman, it's about looking like Clark Kent, as you are in all your mundane normalcy, knowing that there is a restrained power within that can change everything around you. Like the salmon, it's courage that defines a truly creative act because it costs you something. It takes true and sincere courage to show up as you are and allow the world to bear witness. Whether it's releasing a song into a world of critics or voicing your opinion at the meal table of your family, breaking away from the expectation that you have nothing to say, choosing to be intentional about what you do with your creativity is costly. You run the risk of being at the end of rejection, mockery and even worse – indifference. I love the passage in Scripture about when Jesus was praying in the garden of Gethsemane. He was hours away from a horrific death and he called out to God in anxiety and desperation; he was so distressed internally that he was sweating blood. Yet, despite the fear and mounting pressure, he chose to let his friends have a front-row seat and bear witness to his creative act of surrender, calling out to God in the empty, solemn night:

> 'If there's any other way, let it be, and yet . . . not my will but yours be done.'
> (Luke 22.42, my paraphrase)

Words are expensive. I sometimes think of them like buried treasure, trapped in the treacherous terrain of our human experience. There is a quest that costs the brave traveller to find them and the authority to use them. It's one thing to quote the wisdom of people but it's another thing entirely to use the words that you've paid for yourself and the stories you've lived. Often, the people who speak most powerfully say the least, because they are acutely aware of what those words cost them. Like priceless diamonds, forged under unbelievable pressure, their words are spent carefully and intentionally. Our authority comes from our authenticity and, like confession, our creativity reveals what is deepest within. As we express that core truth of our being, it revokes the hold on us of shame.

Shame tries to convince us that there is something inherently wrong with us, as if we're the product that will one day be recalled as a danger to others or as unable to function properly. When we choose to break the cycle of fear–shame–control, when we choose to move from our fear (of being rejected, of not being good enough and so on) with creativity (an honest expression of ourselves), we experience true and lasting freedom. As the patron saint of vulnerability Brené Brown says, 'Vulnerability sounds like truth and feels like courage. Truth and courage aren't always comfortable, but they're never weaknesses.'[13]

There's no promise as to what response you'll get when you express yourself, but that's kind of the point. You don't do it for the response, you do it because a life without it would be so unsatisfying. The export of our creativity doesn't owe us a thing. That mindset shift happened for me the night before my debut album dropped. I thought of all the hours, the money, the vulnerability and the work of my team that had gone into making this work of art and how, at the end, despite the cost, this project owed me nothing. I wasn't owed success, fame, finances or even the time someone had to listen to it. I did it because there was something in me that needed to find expression outside my own body and soul, and anyone who chose to listen was giving me a gift I wasn't entitled to. I think that's why I resonate so deeply with the Hebrew story of creation. It tells us that after God created the land, sea and sky, he announced how good it was and then he rested. That sequence of events lays out the most incredible process for our creativity.

Intention

Once again, it's not a matter of whether we are creative or not but what we choose to do with our creativity that's important. It's not whether you have the capacity to create, it's whether you choose to be courageous with what you have, to create. The Hebrew story in Genesis paints the image of a divine artist who has a vision for a new world (literally) and designs with structure and aesthetic, form and flare, the environment for life to be birthed and sustained. It had to begin somewhere and somehow and the poem records that it all began with a word, a phrase in fact: 'Let there be light.' The biggest struggle I see in people wanting to find a form for an expression of themselves is getting started. For some reason it seems that we require perfection before we can participate and so we stay static, at the starting block, while the gunshot sound reverberates around our mind. I understand the feeling, I've been there more times than I can count, but I've learnt along the way, through confession, writing songs, working on this book even, that the good stuff happens en route. Like a pilgrimage, the destination is only there to give you the motivation to pack your bags, map your route and start walking. Your intention, whatever it is, is like the destination of the pilgrim, has the power to energize and influence you, but it's not there to overwhelm you. Our intention is simply the invitation we need to begin and discover what it is that we are truly making as we do it. I like to imagine that when God spoke the earth into being, the awe-inspiring mountains and delicate flowers were happy accidents and welcomed mistakes made along the way. Ask any artist how their favourite pieces came to be and I guarantee that you'll hear a story about giving way to process rather than a perfectly executed plan. Just begin, break the silence, break the ground, plant a seed and let it grow.

Celebration

Genesis tells us that after God finished making all we see around us, he celebrated. He announced that it was good and revelled in what he had made. I love that image and I've tried to adopt it in my process. I find it a lot easier to celebrate others than myself. I think that comes from internalized doubt and the age-old fear that I'm fooling everyone with what I make, that I'm really not any good, have no idea what I'm doing and at some point someone is going to blow the lid on this whole thing and reveal me for the fraud I am. Taking time to celebrate my creations, simply stepping back and speaking out the phrase 'This is really good', has been so healing. It brings a level of integration and harmony into the chaos of self-doubt and comparison. Also, I've realized that there is a direct connection between my ability to celebrate myself and being able to receive it from others.

My wife is incredible at getting people gifts. We have a big family and she never misses a birthday, anniversary or occasion to buy someone something significant. I think she loves the dignity that receiving a gift can give people. It communicates the worth you place on them and how well you know them. Imagine buying a Christmas present for a loved one, a gift that you invested in and cost you, yet the first thing the person does is throw it away; that's what happens when we can't receive the celebration of others. We dismiss a genuine gift of affection and encouragement that no one owed us in the first place.

Celebrating your creative expression also sustains its impact. The longer you're able to recognize the goodness in what you made, the longer you're able to sustain its life in the world. If you can't stay in the room with your own creativity, why should others? If you can't look at your paintings and address them as 'really good', why should others? It would be unsettling to go to some friends for dinner and, while you're tucking into their home-cooked meal, watch them eat a takeaway because they can't stomach their own cooking. Practising the art of celebration is both healing and empowering. It soothes the wounds of shame and it paves a runway for more creative expression in our life.

Restoration

Finally, after creating with intention and acknowledging that creation with celebration, the story of Genesis tells us that God rested. To return to an image I mentioned earlier, I think of rest as the margins around the page of a book I'm reading. The words matter but without the margins they would run into one another and be senseless. When I rest, I create order and context around everything else I do. I don't rest as a reward, nor to gain something, but to return to the original expression of human design: I am a being not a 'doing'. I am not a tool in the belt of a workman but a picture in the wallet of my Father. God doesn't get me out to use me but to enjoy me. Rhythms of rest, especially in a time of work and creative output, return me to those truths.

Every morning I wake up before my wife and daughter, simply to enjoy and be in silence. I read, pray and meditate. I acknowledge that only in silence can I hear my truest inner voice which helps me to remain integrated and honest. After that, we go to the gym and my wife and I take turns in playing with our daughter while the other works out. Breaking a sweat and experiencing the power and limitations of my body are an expression of rest for me, connecting me deeply to myself and the Creator of my body. Only after that do I look at my phone and begin the day's work. Every Saturday is a 'selah' or Sabbath period for my family. The laptops stay closed, the phones stay off and we enjoy margin. That looks like a slow morning (as much as you can have with a 1-year-old), reading books, smoking a Nicaraguan cigar, going for walks, feasting, watching films, singing songs together on my beaten-up guitar and generally just being with one another. Rest reminds me of nuance. In the space that isn't driven by agendas, consumption, hustle and productivity, I find there's more opportunity to discover the subtle differences in the shade of meaning, expression or sound. That's where my favourite creativity comes from, when I give attention to the spaces between the blocks I build my life with; that's where I find the melodies that stick, the thoughts I pursue and the phrases that hit home. The bombardment of information and entertainment we're used to doesn't leave much space for nuance and results in a sincere lack of original thought.

I think rest relates to our identity much more than we realize. Where we live from says a lot about what we believe about ourselves. If we live from a state of drivenness and ambition (which I have done), we're likely pursuing the fulfilment of an inner sense of lack or longing. To live from rest is to acknowledge that nothing 'out there' will truly fulfil 'in here'. There's a phrase I've seen bandied around, especially among entrepreneurs: 'never not working'. It sounds admirable and dedicated, but I think it would be the last thing any of us would want our friends and family to say of us when we're gone: 'My dad/friend/brother was always working.' The compass that leads me away from the tyranny of being busy and burning out is, 'How do I want those I love most to remember me?' Ultimately, it's as a man who was where he was, present, available, grateful and loving. Those words shape my working day and week and provide the passion and conviction I need to say 'no' to protect my soul.

10

I am a temple

'The Revolution Will Not Be Televised.'
(Title of song by Gil Scott-Heron)

A few years back, I was the support act on a pretty big tour. It was ten nights around the UK, about 3,000 people a show, and I was in my element. People weren't there to see me but that didn't matter. I love being on stage, I love sharing songs and poems, creating an atmosphere and inviting people into a moment outside their normal lives; there's holy electricity in it for me. There's a certain energy, a cocktail of nerves and expectation, that fills your body, the sense you're about to do something that matters and it's somehow transcendent of the moment you're in. It takes thousands of hours honing the craft and practising the piece, but when you finally get up there to do it, despite all the people watching and the attention towards you, surprisingly it feels like it's just as much about everybody else. Like cooking a meal for your friends, you were the one in the kitchen, but when it comes to putting the dishes down on the table, it's a shared act and a collective experience. I feel that way about performing. The songs and poems and sermons belong to each person in the room when they leave my lips, a gift I get to give away over and over again. One of the best things about being on tour, beyond the shows, is discovering the cities you visit, even here in the UK. The places I love the most I've fallen for while exploring before we load in the gear or during a post-show ramble through the city streets.

One afternoon I had some time to kill before my soundcheck, so I looked up what the city had to offer. I was in Lincoln and the cathedral was a must – it didn't disappoint. The interior architecture is overwhelming. The arched ceiling seems eternal, with stoic columns holding it in place. Sunlight pierces through the stained glass, fracturing in multiple colours and directions, illuminating the dark corners and stone pathways. The staggering feat of engineering and design almost takes your breath away, it is truly a sight to behold. I walked around in a daze of wonder and awe, trying to fathom how someone had the inspiration to envision such a masterful expression of creativity. Not only that, but how did they construct it, how was it built, stone upon stone, before the luxuries of modern tech and construction we have today?

As I was strolling around the cathedral, I looked down to see a bronze slab beneath my feet that read: 'Construction commenced here in 1072 and continued in several phases throughout the High Middle Ages.'

That blew my mind. I began listing off the centuries that this incredible structure had stood through and all these stone walls had seen: the rise and fall of empires, the birth of nations, wars and revolution. Sitting down in the chapel adjacent to the main hall, the ancient words of the apostle Paul began ringing out in my mind: 'Do you not know that your bodies are temples of the Holy Spirit? . . . You are not your own' (1 Corinthians 6.19).

I've known that verse my whole life, but there was something about meditating on it there and then that made it suddenly unfamiliar and filled me with reverence. It was as if the word was being made flesh and I was finally realizing the urgency and importance of what Paul was speaking of. I suppose being there I had a sense of the image Paul had in mind when he wrote those words. The Jews' Temple in Jerusalem represented the physical presence of God in their land; it was vast in size, intricate in detail and design and stood to glorify the Holy. It's what made the Roman destruction of their sacred space so harrowing only six years after Paul's epistle.

Our only first-hand account of the Roman assault on the Temple comes from the Jewish historian Flavius Josephus. Josephus was a former leader of the Jewish Revolt, who had surrendered to the Romans. We join his account as the Romans fight their way into the inner sanctum of the Temple:

> the rebels shortly after attacked the Romans again, and a clash followed between the guards of the sanctuary and the troops who were putting out the fire inside the inner court; the latter routed the Jews and followed in hot pursuit right up to the Temple itself. Then one of the soldiers, without awaiting any orders and with no dread of so momentous a deed, but urged on by some supernatural force, snatched a blazing piece of wood and, climbing on another soldier's back, hurled the flaming brand through a low golden window that gave access, on the north side, to the rooms that surrounded the sanctuary. As the flames shot up, the Jews let out a shout of dismay that matched the tragedy; they flocked

to the rescue, with no thought of sparing their lives or husbanding their strength; for the sacred structure that they had constantly guarded with such devotion was vanishing before their very eyes.[14]

That short account gives one a sense of what the Temple meant to those people of devotion and resistance, and it amplifies the power of Paul's words and what he was trying to communicate all those years ago. I imagine him writing with tears running down his cheeks and fire in his bones as he calls out to the early Church, and it still reverberates today: 'Do you not know? Your body is a temple, you are not your own!'

Whatever you have come to think of yourself, however you've been treated by others and, indeed, however mercilessly you've treated yourself in thought, word and deed, you are where the living presence of the Holy resides. You are where God calls home, a temple fit for divine indwelling, sacred and set apart. You are not the worst thing that has been said about you, nor the most spectacular form in which you've failed, you are a carrier of the Spirit. Like a temple, like that old cathedral I found myself in, you are a host of exaltation, prayer and lamentation, praise and prophecy, refuge and safety for the weary and beaten heart. You are more than you realize and will ever fully comprehend in your own lifetime but you might as well make a start. When we meditate on how we were formed and designed, we should be filled with awe-struck wonder. Contemplation of the way we were created inspires us, in turn, to create. You need look no further than your mirror to find the inspiration to make something out of nothing. My view of humanity is a lofty one: we are more than flesh and bones. In the same way, a house is somehow more than just bricks and mortar once someone calls it home. We are miracles with shadows, equations that don't add up, but still manage to tie our shoelaces.

You have more than 10,000 taste buds and 100,000 chemical reactions occurring in your brain every second. All of your blood vessels stretched out would be around 100 km long. Every second, your body produces 25 million new cells. That means in 15 seconds, you will have produced more cells than there are people in the USA. You perform around 23,000 inhalations and exhalations every single day, and your eyes can distinguish 10 million different colours. Pound for pound, your bones are stronger than steel. A block of bone the size of a matchbox can support up to 18,000 pounds of weight and, if you think you won't remember that, your brain has a memory capacity that is the equivalent of more than 4 terabytes on a hard drive!

When we explore our unique and intricate design, we realize the excellence with which the Divine created us and become slowly more and more awakened to the potential for excellence in the creativity, thought, understanding and expression that can come from within. There is a reason that the cathedral was designed the way it was: excellence honours God and it inspires people. So it is with our lives. Could it be that God is using us, living, breathing, walking temples, to rebuild what empires have sought to tear down and destroy. The Roman Empire, as mighty and powerful as it was, is nothing compared to the spirit of empire in the human heart. The ego-driven life seeks to build for its own glory, conquest and gain, leaving a path of destruction in its wake. You've felt it in your workplace, school and social gatherings – the clawing for significance and personal glory, the grasping for attention through shallow ambition at the expense of inner peace. Jesus revealed that Caesar can reign within us all, and the way to overthrow an empire isn't through violent rebellion but the ushering in of a kingdom built on righteousness, peace and joy. As Gil Scott-Heron said so prophetically, the revolution won't be televised, because it is a movement of people simply living their lives, sowing love where there is hatred, forgiveness where there is hurt, faith in the midst of cynicism and despair, light where there is darkness, and sober joy despite unexplainable sorrow.

I think Jesus' sermon on the mount could be called 'how to start a revolution', because it outlines a stark and challenging manifesto for living a counter-cultural existence. His teachings show us that the only way to truly deal with the heart of a matter, however large, however practical, is to begin with healing matters of the heart. His kingdom wasn't revealed through mighty splendour and arrogant displays of power, but in recognizing the need to steward our souls, mining our hearts, as the Psalmist said, for anything that disturbs the shalom, and living a life that radically displays sacrificial love and compassion.

Paul didn't know that less than a decade later, the Temple he was speaking about would be burnt to the ground, but somehow it makes it an even more provocative, prophetic and poetic charge. Rebuild what the empire destroyed, live a life that is worthy of the manner in which you were made. You were not designed as some throwaway, here today, gone tomorrow tent shelter, but as a testimony to what God was doing in this day to be told for generations to come and as a means of awakening others to the wonder of being themselves.

The last tour I went on in the UK began in Newcastle and the day before the first show, I went to spend time in a prison nearby. I played some songs and performed poetry for the guys in there doing time and then I led them through a writing workshop. What was staggering to me during those hours was their fervour and passion to create. Some of them were doing life sentences and would likely never live to see the outside world again, yet the opportunity to make something new, regardless of who would ever hear it, restored dignity and empowered them to see their lives as more than what had happened in their past. Their pieces were honestly beautiful – raw, emotional, rugged. As I listened to them perform, I was reminded of a quote I love from an architect called Norman Foster. He said, 'As an architect, you design for the present, with an awareness of the past and for a future which is essentially unknown.'[15]

That is what we do every time we make space to make something new. We mark the present, the moment we find ourselves in, we honour the past and its part in our story, but we birth something to grow into a future that will evolve beyond us. I'm convinced that when we create, when we recognize that what is in us needs to go somewhere, we fulfil our purpose, as both architects and temples. We stand like a cathedral in a tired and war-torn town, speaking of an ancient story, long forgotten. When we put our hands to work, in labour and creation, we testify to the land that is to come, the world still unravelling before us. When we make something new, from writing songs to baking bread, from building bridges across rivers to building bridges in our relationships, we evoke the testimony of resurrection and we celebrate the death of death; we reveal that the story isn't over and we're only just getting started.

I am a Temple,
A walking sanctuary of God's indwelling,
Where I am present, his presence permeates
    the present,
I have both feet on the earth with my heart hidden
    in heaven,
I've got God's dream in my bloodstream and carry
    worship as a weapon, for we walk beyond
    the melody,
Our worship looks like dirty hands, dusty feet and
    arms embracing enemies.
Our praise transcends the music,
For those who worship in spirit and truth always
    have scars to prove it.
So I must align my actions with the words that
    I speak,
How can I praise with my lips and waste more water
    in a day than most drink in a week?
The weak will be strong, every person is Divine
    property, so it's everybody's problem over a
    billion still live in poverty.
We walk with the authority, of a King who left
    his throne,

To meet the broken in their story, saying you are
    not alone,
There's room at the table and space in the home,
Grace has redefined the state you thought shaped the
    way you'd be known.
So, the Good news is good news, for parched ground
    and parched lips,
For the forgotten and unseen the uncrowned
    and unhinged,
Love doesn't hide behind Extravagance,
If it's heaven-sent it walks among the poor, that's why
    we treat them with holy reverence.
This is New Testament.
God has broken every box and bumper
    sticker sentiment,
Jesus is the evidence the four walls have fallen
    down – we are the walking temple, those who
    represent his temperament.
I believe we are on the precipice and the revolution
    won't be televised, you'll see it in your
    neighbours' lives,
The transformation of society as we wake up and
    come alive,
And bridge the space and break the walls that
    separate the human race,
Now's the time to sound the call and be the change
    we're waiting for.
(The author)

A closing benediction

May you follow your curiosity as you once did as
    a child,
May it lead you where the wild things grow, and may
    you know,
That you are not the summary of your worst days nor
    your best,
You are neither you're failures nor your success,
But the unveiling of a soul, born in awestruck
    wonder and lament.
May you speak, not simply to be heard but to
    birth worlds
That reverberates for generations, like carvings,
    etched into old trees
May the sound of your life, perceived, live beyond
    these passing seasons,
Echoing eternal truths, received by your children's,
    children's children.
May you confess without hesitation,
May the voice of mercy, like the waters
    of baptism,
Wash you in forgiveness, reconciled with what has
    always been true,
May you be reminded of something you once knew,
You are loved without reservation and you are loved
    without condition.
May you in turn become an instrument of peace,
A sound of restoration, a song of true forgiveness,

Heard by the underserving, a witness to the exiled
    and the thief.
May you walk this earth with bare feet,
For all the ground beneath is holy,
May you say that 'Surely God is in this place and I
    knew it',
Beholding the sacred nature of each moment.
May you know friendship in this life
Waking you to wonder, keeping you from
    the slumber
Of despair and indifference,
May you set sail upon uncharted waters, through the
    chaos and the void
With courage and intention finding worlds not yet
    discovered and enjoyed,
May you build a sacred temple with the rubble
    and remains,
To testify that what was lost will rise and live again.
(The author)

Acknowledgements and gratitude

I can't actually believe that I've made it to this part of the book. I started thinking about this final section before I wrote the first chapter, which really makes no sense. I suppose I knew then, as I do now, that the only way I was going to finish this work would be through leaning upon and learning from the gracious friends who walk beside me. Whatever happens with these pages, whoever gets to read them and however far they reach, it's been such a gift to me to be able to write them. The journey of writing has taken me back through the last decade and revealed to me once again what a messy and miraculous journey my life has been. I'm sure you can say the same. In many respects this book is an ode to those memories and all the people who have made them with me, so bear with me. This might go on a bit but, hey, it's my first book and there's no Oscar music to nudge me off stage!

Let me begin with my day one. My ride or die. The Bonny to my Clyde, the Ashanti to my Ja Rule, the Cleopatra to my Antony. Kara Ann Marie, ladies and gentlemen! Thank you for being my best friend, for showing me a better way to live, for giving me a new lens through which to see the world, for helping me live from my heart and for teaching me to walk slowly enough to see the bush ablaze. I've grown up beside you and I am who I am because of your presence in my life. Every night I got to sleep with the woman of my dreams lying next to me.

Acknowledgements

To my daughter and best mate, Eden. Our morning walks have reminded me what it's all about. You fill our home with joy, curiosity and adventure. I'll follow you anywhere. 'I had a dream of you, so you're a dream come true, I never thought Eden would be as real as you.'[16]

To Loretta, one of my closest friends, who just happens to be my manager. This book wouldn't have happened without you. You've trusted, encouraged and facilitated my dreams and ideas from the beginning, bringing integrity, honesty and valour at every turn. You're a gift to me and my girls and I am so glad you're in our lives.

To Elizabeth Neep, who commissioned and edited this book. You saw the statue in the stone of my stories and countless different versions of what this project could be. Thank you for your grace, patience and willingness to persevere with me. I've loved working with you and feel so humbled to be a part of the Form adventure.

To my parents – thank you for giving me the space to become who I am, for never trying to clip the wings of my dreams and for modelling humility and grace like I've found nowhere else. I love you both.

To my sisters – thank you for being so supportive and genuinely interested and invested in what I do. You're still the people I am most excited to share my work with. I am in awe of how you live your lives – you three are my heroes. To Ed and Sam, the brothers I never had, thank you for how you both, in completely different ways, have taught me about becoming a strong and steadfast man, a kind and generous husband and a loving, intentional dad. I'm so grateful for you both.

To Ray, Val and Ryan – if I was you, I don't think that I would have trusted my daughter or sister to a teenager from 3,000 miles away, whose dream was to be a rapper, but you did and I couldn't be more grateful. Thank you for teaching me about board games, big breakfast and the beauty of a family that weathers every storm and celebrates every feast! I love you all.

The family – that dear octopus from whose tentacles we never quite escape, nor, in our inmost hearts, ever quite wish to.[17]

To my friends – I know that sounds vague but if you're reading this wondering if it includes you, then it most likely does. I feel much of my work is plagiarism of sorts, not of some distant icon but of those whose lives I brush against. The way you, my friends, live and love has been much of the fuel for my creative endeavours. I am endlessly inspired by you. I wish I could have written you all into these pages – trust me, I tried!

To Jon and Will, my band of brothers. Thank you for friendship, for the laughter and the depth. I am so grateful to experience life both in the trenches and at the feast table with you. Which reminds me, one of you owes me lunch. Here's to being young men together again.

To Esther, my dear friend, I miss you so much. Thank you for trusting me with your dreams and for giving Kara and me the honour of a lifetime, being your friends. You taught us that all shall be well, even when it wasn't, and I can't wait to write songs with you again, I know we will.

To my Orphan No More community – what an eclectic and eccentric gathering we are. Having the opportunity to walk the path alongside you all this past decade has been heaven on earth, even when we've had to go through hell together. Thank you for giving me the opportunity to taste just how sweet true community can be, in all its messy glory. We're just getting started.

To the family at Life Church Bath, thank you for letting an immature and often ignorant twenty-something preach, pastor and pursue the way of Jesus with you all. My life has been so deeply shaped through the stories I've lived alongside you.

Last, but by no means least, to Mahinda Deegalle, the monk in the laundrette, thank you for listening that day, for taking time to talk and for sparking within me a holy curiosity. I'm still following it to this day.

Notes

1 Carl Sagan, *Cosmos* (New York: Random House, 1980).

2 Quoted in Victor Goertzel and Mildred G. Goertzel, *Cradles of Eminence* (Boston, MA: Little Brown & Co., 1962), p. 248.

3 Abraham Pais, *Subtle Is the Lord: The Science and the Life of Albert Einstein* (Oxford: Oxford University Press, 1982), p. 5.

4 John Cage, *Silence: Lectures and Writings* (Middletown, CT: Wesleyan University Press, 1961), p. 8.

5 Steven Pressfield, *The War of Art: Break through the Blocks and Win Your Inner Creative Battles* (New York: Black Irish Entertainment LLC, 2012).

6 'Disappointment', from David Whyte, *Consolations: The Solace, Nourishment and Underlying Meaning of Everyday Words* (Langley, WA: Many Rivers Press, 2015), © David Whyte.

7 Elizabeth Barrett Browning, from 'Aurora Leigh'.

8 John of the Cross, *Ascent of Mount Carmel*, Book 3, Chapter III, para. 4, trans. E. Allison Peers (New York: Image Books, 1962), p. 195.

9 Julian of Norwich, *Revelations of Divine Love*, in Richard Foster and James Bryan Smith, *Devotional Classics* (San Francisco, CA: HarperOne, 1990), p. 7.

10 Henri Nouwen, *Bread for the Journey: A Daybook for Wisdom and Faith* (London: Darton, Longman & Todd, 1997).

11 *The Holocaust Twin Who Forgave the Nazis*, BBC Ideas, 2021.

12 Stephen Hawking, *Brief Answers to the Big Questions* (New York: Bantam Books, 2018), p. 38.

13 Brené Brown, *Daring Greatly: How the Courage to be Vulnerable Transforms the Way We Live, Love, Parent, and Lead* (New York: Gotham Books, 2012), p. 37.

14 Gaalya Cornfield (ed.), *Josephus: The Jewish War* (Grand Rapids, MI: Zondervan, 1982); Victor Duruy, *History of Rome*, vol. V (London: Kegan, Paul, Trench & Co,, 1883).

15 TED talk: Norman Foster on Green Architecture, 21 November 2015.

16 From my song 'Dreaming of Eden', released in November 2021 on *Orphan No More*.

17 Dodie Smith, *Dear Octopus*, play first performed at the Queen's Theatre, London, 14 September, 1938.